Making Bent Willow Furniture

Brenda & Brian Cameron

Storey Publishing

Acknowledgments

Bent willow furniture making is an old craft kept alive by individuals and families who passed the skill down through generations. Driven by a need for basic low-cost furniture, the craft flourished in mining towns of the West in the late 1800s and again during the Depression era. Its current popularity may be driven more by an appreciation for natural and ecologically friendly furniture than by economic necessity.

Our sincere thanks to Joe Elders for sharing his knowledge with a new generation of apprentices, and to Don King for sharing his design ideas and techniques.

Brenda and Brian Cameron

The mission of Storey Publishing is to serve our customers by publishing practical information that encourages personal independence in harmony with the environment.

Edited by Deborah Balmuth and William Overstreet
Cover design by Rob Johnson, Johnson Design
Cover photographs by Jerry Pavia
Text design by Mark Tomasi
Text production by Erin Lincourt
Photographs by Jerry Pavia, except on page 11
Line drawings by Rick Daskam

The information in this book is true and complete to the best of our knowledge. All recommendations are made without guarantee on the part of the author or Storey Publishing. The author and publisher disclaim any liability in connection with the use of this information. For additional information please contact Storey Publishing, 210 MASS MoCA Way, North Adams, MA 01247.

Storey books are available for special premium and promotional uses and for customized editions. For further information, please call 1-800-793-9396.

Printed in the United States by R.R. Donnelley
10 9 8 7 6

Library of Congress Cataloging-in-Publication Data

Cameron, Brenda, 1953–
    Making bent willow furniture / Brenda and Brian Cameron.
       p.   cm. — (The rustic home series)
    Includes index.
    ISBN 1-58017-048-X (pbk. : alk. paper)
    1. Wicker furniture.   2. Furniture making.   I. Cameron, Brian, 1951– .   II. Title.   III. Series
TT197.7.C35   1998
684.1'06—dc21

98-12990
CIP

Contents

Introduction

Gypsies crossed my grandfather's farm in Oklahoma twice a year on their annual migration south in the winter and back north in the summer. Grandpa let them camp down by the creek where they often cut willow and made "stick furniture," as grandpa called it. They sold their stick furniture to local folks, and it became a common sight on farmhouse porches and lawns.

The simplicity and rustic beauty of this furniture intrigued me at an early age. Replicating these designs as closely as I could, I hammered together my own willow tables and chairs to furnish our old tree house. Although my furniture was more crude, it gave me a great sense of freedom and independence to build something for myself. My friends and family marveled at my ingenuity, and some of them offered to help me cut willow. Sufficiently encouraged, I furnished tree houses for miles around. For years after, I searched in vain for someone who could instruct me in all aspects of this craft.

◀ Gypsy Willow Loveseat (p. 72)

In the spring of 1991, in a small town in Oklahoma, I was fortunate enough to find a bent willow master through an ad he had placed in the local newspaper.

Joe Elders had been making bent willow furniture for sixty-four years, since he was fifteen years old. Joe's older brother learned the craft while harvesting wheat in

▼ Grandma's Fan Double Bed Headboard (p. 100) with Log Cabin Planter Boxes (p. 120)

▲ Large Hanging
Basket (p. 49)

Colorado and taught it to his siblings. The brothers used nails from burned-down structures and willows gathered along Ridesville Creek in Alabama to make bent willow chairs, settees, and tables. They sold their rustic furniture from a wagon in the streets of Birmingham and Huntsville, Alabama, and in Nashville, Tennessee, in the early 1930s. At that time, a set of bent willow furniture (settee, chair, and table) sold for just $2.

▲ Magazine Rack (p. 32),
Lounger (p. 82), and Plant
Stand (p. 36)

At age 79, Joe patiently taught me to build the "gypsy willow" furniture he so loved. In the warm spring sunshine, we gathered black willow from barrows and ditches along the freeway near his home and built a set of willow furniture that I cherish to this day.

Since meeting Joe, I've found a few others who share my love for willow. Don King is an artist and skilled craftsman who builds willow masterpieces in Challis, Idaho. He brings a contemporary flair to his work, and his unique willow and rustic furniture designs are displayed in museums and fine furniture stores across the United States. His work inspires, and reflects the limitless potential of this seemingly simple craft (see page 11 for an example of his work).

▼ Southwestern Mirror (p. 113): frame can be used to hold mirror tiles, photographs, or artwork

▲ Tulip Mirror Frame (p. 107)

History

Varied, creative rustic furniture designs are found in many cultures worldwide. Perhaps the oldest example is a tenth-century painting of a Chinese scholar enthroned on a chair made of gnarled branches.

Rustic furniture was a popular landscape element in many European gardens in the Victorian era. Physicians of the time believed contact with nature improved both health and spirit. Ailing aristocrats who convalesced in the country built their own nature gardens at home and equipped them with rustic furniture. In sharp contrast to the formal style of the time, these rustic gardens provided a momentary escape to unbridled nature.

In the United States, rustic willow furniture was made for many generations by families in the south and Amish families in the east and midwest. Traveling bands of gypsies helped spread the craft throughout the West, as they made furniture for their own use and sold it when they moved. These early craftsmen developed

▲ Children's Chair (p. 58)
and Children's Table (p. 54)

unique styles that still exist today. The Adirondack style is rustic, the Amish style is sturdy and functional, and the Victorian and gypsy styles are functional, with decorative flourishes.

In the late 1800s in the United States, bent willow furniture was popularized with all classes. In resorts, it was part of the natural country surroundings that wealthy city dwellers experienced in their quiet retreats. The craft flourished in gold camps and mining towns of the West, its popularity driven by a need for basic low-cost

▲ Small Hanging Basket
(p. 44)

furniture. The staunch pioneers who settled these rugged areas made much of their furniture out of available materials. Because most accessible lumber was used in constructing the mines, willow — a flexible, durable wood undesirable for such construction — was ideally suited for furniture making. The Gypsy Willow Chair (featured on page 10) and Loveseat (featured on page 1) are bent willow designs found in the Idaho mining towns of Custer and Idaho City. They display the creativity and durability of the designs of this period.

For the Love of Willow

The need to "get away from it all" is a common human urge that often leads to the search for a quiet retreat

▼ Decorative Wheelbarrow Plant Stand (p. 124)

surrounded by nature. Underneath the shielding arms of a shady tree, we are able to unravel knotted nerves and experience the peaceful tranquility only Mother Nature can provide. The current popularity of bent willow furniture may derive from our innate need for nature.

If you love trees, it is likely you also will love bent willow furniture. There is something immediately familiar about willow furniture that embraces you and connects your spirit to nature. The look and smell of the wood awakens a deep, peaceful part of the soul. The craft of bent willow furniture allows you to bring the spirit of nature into your home, so you can enjoy it year-round.

Unlike milled lumber, willow is rarely uniform in dimension. Each piece of willow is unique and reflects nature's diversity. As such, each piece of willow furniture is different, reflecting the skill and creativity of its builder as well as the unique character of the wood.

◀ Gypsy Willow Chair (p. 64)

▲ Bent willow chair, titled *Ambivalence*, designed and crafted by Don C. King

Get Started!

If you are new to this craft, learn the basic carpentry skills and simple techniques for working with willow discussed in chapters 1 and 2. Then, begin the projects. Soon you'll be able to apply these skills and construction techniques to more intricate designs of your own.

Folks who already understand basic carpentry should review chapters 1 and 2 to learn about willow and the best techniques for this craft. It is our hope that in time you will develop a "willow eye," the ability to choose specific pieces for your project before cutting them from the thicket.

Whether you are a beginner or a skilled carpenter, it is our hope that you will devote many peaceful, pleasurable hours to this craft. If it speaks to your heart, share it with your children and grandchildren and become part of the bent willow tradition.

◀ Quilt Ladder (p. 30)

# CHAPTER 1

Gathering and Preparing Willows

Willows have been used by civilizations throughout the world in many different ways. The symbol for willow is found in Assyrian and Sumerian tablets that date back 4,000 years, and Hippocrates prescribed the white willow in his medical practice around 450 B.C.. Many doctors used an extract from willow bark to treat malaria fevers during the late 1700s. And in the 1890s, willow bark extract became the basic ingredient for aspirin.

Soft, light willow wood made superior charcoal for gunpowder and other uses and served as a popular summer fuel for quick, hot fires. Tannin was made from the bitter bark, and the inner bark of some species was used to make fishing lines. Many native peoples fashioned cradle carriers, snares, fish traps, and baskets from willow twigs.

Where and How They Grow

Willows (genus *Salix*) are distributed from the equator to the Arctic Circle. Hundreds of species exist, with many natural hybrids between closely related species. Most species prefer moist soil, but a few prefer dry. Willows grow in abundance from sea level to the tops of mountain chains, and they vary in size from great trees to low shrubs.

Easy Propagation

Willows propagate very quickly. Species *Salix viminalis* can grow more than 12 feet in one season. A twig stuck into moist soil will grow into a tree. If you set out green willow fence posts, they soon root and grow into trees. Some species have twigs that snap off at the base and then root if they fall on damp ground. Many waterside willows cast their twigs in this way. The stream carries them to shoals and bars, which soon become covered with trees.

Stopping Erosion

Willows provide an immeasurable service in areas where shifting sand and mud banks contribute to erosion. Their growth in these areas helps stabilize the soil and supports wildlife with food and shelter. In damp areas, willow roots drain and improve the soil. Willows have been used to hold together the banks of streams and ditches in Holland and other countries. In the United States, willow shrubs held the banks of the levees that opened the Mississippi channel for navigation. Willows planted along highways that cross rocky, hillside terrain form barriers that help keep rolling rocks off the road.

Common Willow Species

A few willows grow into large trees. The golden osier (*Salix alba* var. *vitellina*), whose yellow limbs are bright in early spring, can be seen in many a fence row across North America. It is also called the white willow of Europe. The Babylonian willow (*Salix babylonica*) is the familiar weeping willow of the Eastern United States. Two of the most ornamental willows, the Wisconsin weeping willow (*Salix × blanda*) and the laurel willow (*Salix pentandra*) are found in many public parks.

Most beginners ask me where they can find willow. Willow grows in abundance from sea level to the tops of mountain chains. Joe Elders, who taught me this craft, gathered willow from gullies and ditches along the freeway. Once you identify the type of willow that grows in your area, you may be surprised to find it growing in your own back yard, in the empty lot next door, or along the irrigation ditch down the street. Farmers and ranchers are usually happy to have you cut willow out of their irrigation ditches, but be sure to secure permission before harvesting willow from private or public lands.

If you are not sure what willow looks like, ask a horticulturist at your local college or a botanist from the nearest Cooperative Extension Service or U.S. Forest Service office. Your local library is also a good source. The following pages describe the features and the location of some of the most common willows.

Balsam Willow
(*Salix balsamifera*)

Features: The balsam willow forms a low shrub with a long stem crowned by a small clump of branches. The broad, oval leaves are blunt on the ends.

Habitat: This willow inhabits cold bogs in the northern states and west to Minnesota.

Bebb's Willow
(*Salix Bebbiana*)

Features: The Bebb's willow, a small tree 10 to 20 feet tall, has a short trunk, downy twigs, and smooth, reddish bark. The oblong leaves, 1 to 3 inches long with short, pointed ends, are dull green on top and whitish or gray underneath. According to some experts, the inner bark makes excellent fishing line.

Habitat: The Bebb's willow prefers dry soil or stream borders. It ranges from central Alaska south to British Columbia, from the Rocky Mountains to southern New Mexico, and east to Newfoundland and Maryland.

Black Willow

(*Salix longipes*)

Features: This species of black willow has a wide, tapering leaf with silvery lining. It grows into a small tree 20 to 30 feet high.

Habitat: *S. longipes* is found in abundance in the Ozark Mountains along rocky banks of streams. It also grows from Washington, D.C., to Florida and west to Missouri and New Mexico.

Black Willow

(*Salix nigra*)

Features: The black willow can grow to be a medium sized tree 50 to 100 feet high but is usually smaller. Its slender twigs are brittle at the base, its bark dark brown, flaky, deeply furrowed, and often shaggy. A distinguishing feature of the foliage is the pair of leaflike, heart-shaped stipules at the base of each leaf. It is the only narrow-leaved willow with foliage uniformly green on both sides. The leaves often curve like a sickle.

Habitat: The black willow grows along the borders of lakes and streams from Newfoundland to Florida, west to the Rocky Mountains, and also in California.

Golden Osier

(*Salix alba* var. *vitellina*)

Features: The golden osier, a venerable-looking tree 40 to 60 feet tall, has a short trunk and spreading top. It features golden yellow twigs and rough gray bark. The oblong, notched leaves, 2 to 4 inches long, taper at both ends. The American equivalent of the European white willow, this variety is one of the most vigorous and useful.

Habitat: The golden osier is found in eastern North America.

Heart Willow

(*Salix cordata*)

Features: The heart willow grows as a shrub in the East, but its Western cousin, *Salix Mackenzieanna,* can be a tree. The pointed leaves bear minute, kidney-shaped stipules throughout the summer.

Habitat: The heart willow grows from the far North to the Rocky Mountains in Idaho and west into California.

Hooker Willow

(*Salix hookeriana*)

Features: Rarely over 30 feet tall, the hooker willow can be distinguished by its hoary twigs. Its broad, oblong leaves are blunt at the tips and downy white underneath.

Habitat: The Hooker willow grows wild in sand dunes and salt marshes from Vancouver Island to southern Oregon.

Missouri Willow

(Salix Missouriensis)

Features: The Missouri willow can grow 50 feet tall with a trunk 1 ½ feet thick. It has thin grey bark with small scales and dark brown wood. The notched leaves, 3 to 6 inches long, taper to a fine point. They are smooth and green on top, pale and a light blue-green color underneath.

Habitat: This willow flourishes in northern Missouri, northeastern Kansas, Nebraska, and western Iowa.

Pacific Willow
(Yellow Willow, Western Black Willow)

(Salix lasiandra)

Features: This widespread willow, a familiar sight along river banks, grows into a small tree or thicket-forming shrub 20 to 50 feet tall. Its bright green leaves are whitish underneath, 4 to 5 inches long, notched, and finely cut-toothed.

Habitat: The Pacific willow grows along river banks and lake shores from British Columbia to California and east into Montana, Colorado, and New Mexico.

Peach-Leaved Willow

(Salix amygdaloides)

Features: An erect, straight-branched tree, the peach-leaf willow typically grows 30 to 40 feet tall but sometimes reaches 70 feet. It has brown scaly bark on thick plates. The 3- to 5-inch leaves, silky smooth and paler underneath, strongly resemble peach tree leaves. This is one of the few willows that grows above medium height.

Habitat: The peach-leaf willow inhabits the borders of streams and lakes from Quebec to British Columbia, south through New York, Missouri, and New Mexico. Although rare in the East, it is common in the Ohio Valley and along streams that flow down the eastern slope of the Rocky Mountains. It is widely cultivated in midwestern landscapes.

Pussy Willow

(Salix discolor)

Features: Although very familiar when immature, this bog willow may not be recognized in leaf. The twigs are usually cut when the little furry catkins peep out in late winter. Florists buy large quantities for decorative arrangements. The mature willow forms a shrub or small tree 25 feet tall with stout purplish-red, downy branchlets. The leaves, 3 to 5 inches long, are scalloped, pointed at both ends, and bright green with a pale or silvery lining.

Habitat: The pussy willow prefers to grow in swamps and along moist hillsides from Nova Scotia to Manitoba and south to Delaware and Missouri.

Sandbar Willow

(Salix fluviatilis)

Features: The sandbar willow grows into either a slender tree, 20 to 30 feet tall, or a bushy shrub. Its silky leaves, yellow-green and lighter on the under side, taper at both ends.

Habitat: The sandbar willow prefers moist soil along streams from Quebec to the Northwest Territory, south to Virginia, Kentucky, and New Mexico.

Scouler or Fire Willow
(Salix scouleriana)

Features: The Scouler willow quickly establishes itself on burned-over areas, so it is often called the fire willow. This species tolerates remarkable temperature extremes, from $-75°F$ ($-59°C$) in winter to $120°F$ ($49°C$) in the summer. It grows into a small tree or shrub, 15 to 50 feet tall, with rounded, compact crown and straight trunk. The leaves are dark green, smooth on top, and whitish with gray or reddish hairs underneath.

Habitat: The Scouler willow grows in clearings and cut or burned-over areas of upland coniferous forests, at elevations up to 10,000 feet, from central Alaska to Manitoba, south to California and New Mexico, and in the Black Hills.

Shining Willow
(Salix lucida)

Features: The shining willow is a small, round-headed tree distinguished by the lustre of its ruddy twigs and the beautiful sheen of its dark green, leathery leaves. Many landscape designs feature it.

Habitat: A native of the North, this willow ranges from Newfoundland westward to Hudson Bay and the Rockies, and southward as far as Pennsylvania and Nebraska.

Silver-Leaved Willow
(Salix sessilifolia)

Features: The small silver-leaved willow is distinguished by its many silky, veined leaves. At maturity the upper surface of the leaves turns pale yellow-green.

Habitat: This is one of the most common willows along the southern coast of California. It also grows along the borders of streams from Puget Sound south to the western slopes of the Sierra Nevada.

Harvesting Willow

Careful harvesting promotes healthier growth of willow thickets and has a low environmental impact since willow propagates very quickly. Fresh twigs left over from your trimmings will sprout new growth if you plant the cut end, about 10 inches deep, in moist soil near the thicket. You should always use sharp cutting tools to harvest willow. Make clean cuts: Never rip or tear the branches or pull the roots out.

Tools for Harvesting Willow

The tools you'll need to harvest willow are probably already in your garden tool shed. Make sure you keep them oiled and sharpened. If you need new tools, buy the best you can afford. The initial expense will pay you back in years of untroubled use.

Pruning Saw. You will use the pruning saw to harvest the larger limbs for frame material. Many types work well, but a model that folds into its handle is easier to pack.

Pruning Shears. Use pruning shears to trim small branches and cut the long thin shoots for flexible benders and back and seat rails. Find a pair that fits comfortably in your hand. Ratchet-action shears will help you cut larger branches as easily as smaller ones.

Measuring Tape. A tape measure will help you cut the right lengths of willow. A retractable tape measure carries nicely on your belt. A plastic dressmaker's tape can be draped around your neck and rolled up to carry in your pocket.

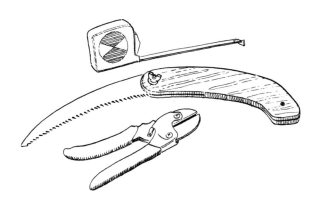

When to Harvest

Willows can be harvested year-round. When you harvest depends on the look you want to achieve in your final piece of furniture. Harvest in fall and winter if you intend to leave the bark on your furniture. The moisture content of the wood is low at that time of the year, which makes the bark tight and minimizes shrinkage as the furniture dries. Also, once the leaves have fallen, you'll find it easier to spot suitable shoots and you'll have less trimming to do.

Harvest in spring and summer if you intend to remove the bark; the higher moisture content makes the bark easy to strip off. Natural willow wood is an attractive light blonde color, or it can be dyed or painted to enhance any decor. Be aware, however, that willow harvested in the spring or summer will often sprout. This is not a problem if you remember to remove the sprouts, but unfinished furniture left on a damp lawn may turn into a willow thicket!

What to Harvest

You will need both seasoned (dry) pieces of willow and green, flexible "bender" pieces, depending on your project design. The seasoned branches are required for frames and support pieces, while the benders are used to create arched pieces.

Always gather more material than you think you will need for your project in case you miscut or break some pieces in the assembly process.

Frame Pieces. The willow branches for the frame should be 1" to 3" in diameter and as tall and straight as possible. These pieces need to be seasoned before they can be used. Plan ahead so you can season them for about 7 days before you build your furniture. To season, stand the pieces against a sunny wall, or lay the pieces out in the

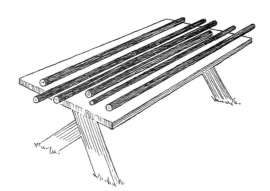

sunshine. Provide good ventilation, and keep the pieces off the ground so they will dry out faster.

Bender Pieces. The green, bender pieces of willow should be ½" to ¾" in diameter, 6 to 8 feet long, and as straight as possible. Once cut, place these pieces cut-end down in a bucket of water to keep them flexible. Leave your bucket of benders in a cool shady spot, but don't let the water freeze. If you don't use them right away, you will probably have to trim off some sprouts before proceeding.

Preparing the Willows

When you are ready to start a project, separate the seasoned frame pieces by diameter, and trim off small nubs or branches. You may also want to sort for color and texture in each diameter. This makes it easier to find a matching piece if you need to. Look for pieces that have distinguishing features, such as an unusual knot or curve, you might want to highlight. Label these pieces for a specific use in the project, making certain the unusual features that caught your eye will be visible.

Limbering Up the Benders

It's easier to work with flexible benders if you limber them up before you attach them. Stretching the wood fibers makes the benders more pliable and much easier to bend. There are several methods; try each and select one that works best for you. Here are a couple of techniques:

❦ Take one end of the bender in each hand and flex it back and forth.

❦ Lay the bender on the floor, then step on one end while you flex the other end. With longer pieces you can walk down the bender while you flex the other end back and forth. Some may break, so be sure to have extra material on hand.

Stripping the Bark

Willow wood has an attractive light blonde color that resembles natural wicker. Plain stripped pieces can be incorporated in your design to create interesting color contrasts, or the stripped pieces can be dyed or painted to enhance your color scheme.

In the spring and summer, when the sap is up in the wood, cut the lengths you need for your design and strip the pieces while they are still green and supple.

Score a line down the length of the limb, being careful not to cut too deeply. The bark should peel off in long strips. These strips can be used to make willow bark baskets.

If you want to dye the wood, it's a good idea to do it right after you strip it. The uniform moisture content of the green wood will give a more even color (see chapter 5 for instructions on dyeing willow).

# CHAPTER 2

Tools and Basic Construction Techniques

The most important thing to remember when building with willow branches is that this is not an exact science: You are not working with sawed, uniform lumber. Before you use a piece of willow, carefully observe its natural bends and bows, then place it to the best advantage in your design. As you build, stand back periodically and look at how the overall shape of your piece is developing, making adjustments as needed. Let the willow be your guide; each cut branch has its own character and shape that will help you create a beautifully curved one-of-a-kind piece.

If you can follow a basic recipe, you can build a willow chair with just five tools: hammer, tape measure, bow saw, pruning shears, and cordless drill. You might consider bringing these tools with you on your next camping or fishing trip. Making a willow chair is a great family project, and the completed piece will add rustic charm to your porch or home. Years from now, you'll look at the chair and fondly remember the fun you had making it — even if the fish weren't biting.

Tools You Will Need

For centuries, willow furniture was built without power tools. Today, many still-functional pieces built in the late 1800s and early 1900s are displayed in museums or housed in private collections. Keep in mind that power tools can be helpful but are not essential for this craft. In fact, you probably already own most of the basic tools:

Hammer. A 16-ounce finish hammer works well. Choose a hammer that you find comfortable.

Marker Pencil. A carpenter's pencil, chalk, or felt-tip markers are best to use on wood so you can see the marks easily.

Tape Measure. The tape measure you took along to harvest willow will be handy in the shop for checking the final length before assembly.

Safety Glasses and Gloves. When working with wood, always protect your eyes from bits of sawdust and flying wood chips, with safety glasses or goggles and wear work gloves anytime you use a sharp tool.

Pruning Saw or Bow Saw. Use a pruning saw or a bow saw to cut framing material to the correct lengths.

Hacksaw. You'll need a hacksaw to cut threaded rod for some of the projects in this book. A blade with 18 teeth per inch is recommended.

Pruning Shears. To trim benders to their final length, use the pruning shears you took along to harvest willow.

Dikes or Side-Cutting Pliers. The dikes or side-cutting pliers can be used to trim nails that may stick out too far.

Jigsaw. An inexpensive jigsaw is used to cut plywood for some of the projects in this book. You might also use a keyhole saw for this task.

Trimming and Shaping Tools. For trimming off small nubs on branches and rounding edges, a block or Surform plane, a rasp, or an all-purpose utility knife with a replaceable blade works well. A rasp or Surform plane can also smooth rough edges, and a half-round rasp will help you round off joints. You can use a flat double-cut steel file to grind off nail tips.

Small Electric Grinder. This handy power tool can be used in place of the double-cut steel file to grind off protruding nails. We use a Dremel tool with a silicon-carbide grinding wheel.

Drill. You'll need a ⅜-inch variable-speed drill with a selection of bits. A cordless drill is handiest because it will let you get into tight places without tangling a cord.

Work Space. Level, unobstructed work space measuring about 8 × 12 feet is desirable. The area should be well ventilated and far away from sources of spark or flame. Work benches can be helpful but aren't essential for building this furniture. If you want to make a temporary, portable workbench, place a sheet of ½-inch or ¾-inch plywood on top of sawhorses.

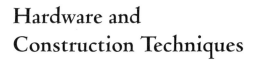

Tips for Drilling

❧ When drilling, place a piece of scrap lumber underneath the piece to prevent damage to the drill and the surface where you are working.

❧ Before you begin drilling, set the site with a nail or punch to prevent the drill from slipping off the mark.

❧ To drill a straight hole, place your hand on the drill with your middle finger on the trigger and your index finger running alongside the drill motor, pointing directly at the hole. Your index finger helps you focus on the target.

❧ If the fastener is to pass completely through the piece of willow, drilling the pilot hole all the way through will help prevent splitting the willow.

❧ Before drilling any holes in a piece, read all instructions for the project carefully. Be sure you know where the piece will go and how it will be fastened before proceeding.

Hardware and Construction Techniques

The simple lines of bent willow furniture enhance its visual appeal. Fortunately for novices, weekend do-it-yourselfers, and anyone else interested in creating unique decorative and functional pieces, no prior building experience is necessary to learn this craft. Before attempting a project, do familiarize yourself with the helpful information that follows and review the information on gathering and cutting willow in chapter 1.

Fasteners

To attach frame and support pieces to each other, use either galvanized 6d and 16d ring-shank nails or bronze-colored 2- and 3-inch deck screws. These ribbed fasteners won't rust and will hold well in both seasoned and green wood. The silver-colored galvanized nails blend in nicely with gray bark, while the deck screws give a nice gold patina to your design. (The projects in this book usually call for 6d and 16d nails.)

Use smaller ribbed paneling nails — 1 inch and 1 ⅝ inch — to attach benders and seat and back rails.

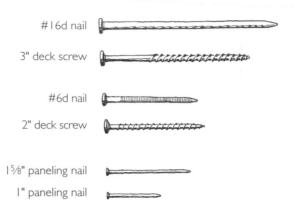

Tips for Using Fasteners

❖ In your work area keep small labeled containers of each size nail you plan to use.

❖ Drill pilot holes for the fasteners to minimize splitting as the wood dries. Use a drill bit 25 percent smaller in diameter than the fastener you plan to use. Drill the hole a bit deeper into the willow than the fastener will go so you can easily drive the fastener in farther after the wood dries and shrinks.

❖ If you double nail a piece, stagger the nails so you won't split the willow ends.

❖ It will take approximately 3 to 6 months for green wood to dry completely after assembly. After that, check all the joints and drive in any nails that may have popped out.

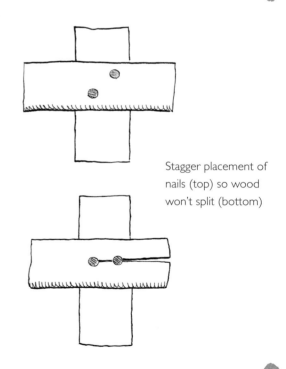

Stagger placement of nails (top) so wood won't split (bottom)

Templates

Willow benders are springy and sometimes hard to shape evenly as you form the arched back for a piece, as in the Gypsy Willow Chair. To get a nice round or pear shape, I recommend using a plywood template.

Making a Template. Cut a template the exact size and shape you want for the back from ¾-inch plywood, and temporarily fasten or clamp it onto the frame. Arch the innermost flexible bender around the edge of the template and nail it to the frame — *not* to the template. The plywood template will hold the bender's shape while you attach the rest of the benders. You can remove the template when all the benders are in place.

A rounded plywood template allows you to create an arched back for the Gypsy Willow Chair (p. 64).

Using a Routed Template

A routed template can be used to create unique designs, such as Don King's chair (see photo on page 11). The curved shape for the individual benders in this piece was first drawn on a piece of plywood. Then a half-round channel was routed into the plywood following the drawn line, using a bit the diameter of the benders. The channel was cut long enough to accommodate the longest bender required by the design. The benders were placed in the channel and weighted or clamped into place until they dried. Although quite flexible when green, willow is rigid and holds its shape well once cured, after which you can remove it from the template.

If you intend to strip the bark or dye the wood for a design made with a routed template, do so before you attach the pieces to the template. Wetting the wood after it has cured in the template may cause it to lose some of its shape.

Joints

There are several types of joints you can use in constructing willow furniture, the three most common being the T-joint, the corner joint, and the spliced joint. For added strength, glue the joints before you nail them. A polyurethane glue is particularly useful for gluing green or partially green wood.

Square T-Joint. The squared T-joint is the most common. It is formed by butting the end of one limb against a crosspiece. Cut the limb square across and nail it to the crosspiece.

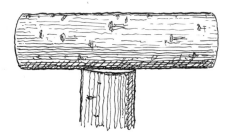

Rounded T-Joint. When you become more experienced, you may want to try a rounded T-joint, which is stronger and more attractive than the square T-joint. To make a rounded T-joint, cut a shallow V into the butt end of the limb with a

hacksaw, and then round the V with a coarse rat-tail or half-round file so that it fits the shape of the crosspiece. *Be aware, however, that the rounded T-joint shortens the length of the piece by the depth of the notch you cut.* Always cut a piece longer by the depth of the notch to make up the difference.

Corner Joint. A corner joint is really just two more-or-less perpendicular T-joints with a common crossbar. This type of joint may be used to attach the rungs to the legs of a chair, for example. Stagger the nails so you don't split the wood.

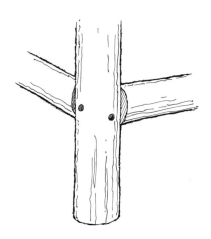

Spliced Joint. Spliced joints can be used to lengthen back or arm benders that are not quite long enough. Lay the benders beside each other on a flat surface and simultaneously angle-cut both pieces, at least 2 inches from the ends. This way the angles should match each other. Glue the joint and nail the pieces together. Be sure to position the joint where the spliced bender will not curve, thereby minimizing pressure on the splice.

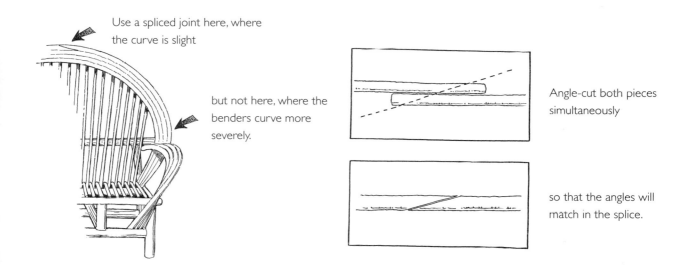

Use a spliced joint here, where the curve is slight

but not here, where the benders curve more severely.

Angle-cut both pieces simultaneously

so that the angles will match in the splice.

# CHAPTER 3

# Beginning Projects

f you are a beginner, read chapters 1 and 2 and assemble the basic tools and equipment before starting your first project. Those chapters introduce simple techniques for working with willow that you'll need to know to build the projects in this chapter. Once you master these basic skills, you can try more creative and intricate designs.

Tools and Hardware for Projects in This Chapter

- Dikes or side cutting pliers
- Drill with $1/16$", $3/32$", and $1/8$" bits, plus a 1" paddle bit
- Electrician's tape
- Flat double-cut file
- Hammer
- Jigsaw
- Marker (felt-tip, chalk, or pencil)
- Nails: 6d, 8d, 16d
- Paneling nails: 1", $1^{5}/8$"
- Pruning or bow saw
- Pruning shears
- Rasp or Surform plane
- Safety glasses and gloves
- Tape measure
- Utility knife

Remember, it's easier to work with flexible benders if you limber them up before you attach them. Stretching the wood fibers makes the benders more pliable and much easier to bend. (See page 20 for instructions.)

The wood on any of the projects in this chapter is perfectly fine left natural and unfinished, unless otherwise noted. However, if you wish to change the color or look of the piece, try one of the finishes described in chapter 5.

The children's chair (page 58) and table (page 54) are two beginning projects that can be great fun to build with young helpers!

Trimming and Tightening

The following should be done for all bent willow furniture projects:

- ❧ Cut off and file down any nail tips that stick out too far, and smooth the rough edges.

- ❧ Let willow pieces season for 3 to 6 weeks out of direct sunlight.

- ❧ After 3 to 6 months, check all the joints. Drive in any nails that may have popped out as the wood dried. Any glued joints may need additional gluing.

Quilt Ladder

I first saw this simple, very functional rustic ladder in Arizona. It leaned against the side of a stucco fireplace. A very colorful quilt hung from the top rung and herbs were tied to dry on the two bottom rungs. I thought about grandma's quilts I had stored in the attic and decided this would be a great way to display them.

Materials				
Part	Quantity	Diameter	Length	Type of Wood
rails	2	2"	72"	seasoned
top rung	I	I ½"	16"	seasoned
center rung	I	I ½"	cut to fit	seasoned
bottom rung	I	I ½"	24"	seasoned

1. Preparing the Rails

Starting from the small (top) end of each rail, measure and mark points along the side of the rail at 12", 28", and 44". Keep the paired marks in line with each other and in the center of the limbs. Drill ⅛" pilot holes straight through the center of the rail at each point.

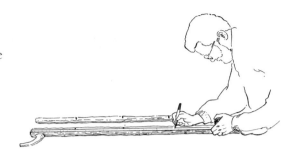

2. Attaching the Rungs

Drill a ⅛" pilot hole in the center of each end of the top and bottom rung pieces. (Remember to make your pilot holes slightly deeper than the fastener will set.) Place the top rung between the rails at the 12" marks and nail with 16d nails. At the 44" marks do the same with the bottom rung.

Measure between the rails at the 28" mark and cut the center rung to fit. Drill a ⅛" pilot hole in the center of each end of this rung. Secure it as you did the other rungs.

Round the top and bottom edges of the rails with a rasp or Surform plane.

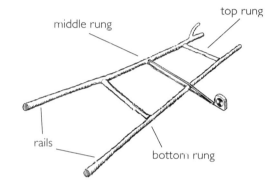

middle rung
top rung
rails
bottom rung

Safety Tip

When drilling, always wear safety glasses or, even better, goggles to prevent loose pieces of wood from flying into your eyes.

Magazine Rack or Garden Tool Caddy

This has been one of the most versatile willow pieces we've built. It's a magazine rack or a garden caddy all right, but we also use it as an incentive for getting children to pick up after themselves. We give each of the grandchildren a willow caddy and send them off to gather up their scattered toys. It works great!

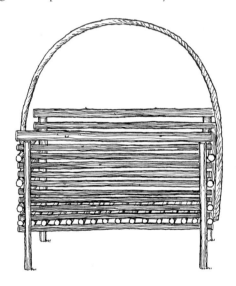

Materials				
Part	Quantity	Diameter	Length	Type of Wood
bottom frame	2	¾"	8"	seasoned
	2	¾"	18"	seasoned
	16 to 18	½"	9¼"	seasoned
legs	4	¾"	12"	seasoned
rails	2	¾"	18"	seasoned
side frames	18	½"	17½"	seasoned
end pieces	6	¾"	12"	seasoned
handle	1	¾"	48"	flexible bender

1. Assembling the Bottom Frame

Round the edges of all the bottom frame pieces with a rasp or Surform plane.

Measure in 1¼" from each end of the two 18" pieces. Mark the four sides and then drill two ¹⁄₁₆" in-line pilot holes through each piece. Also drill a pilot hole in the center of the ends of each 8" piece. Then, nail the four pieces together with 1⅝" paneling nails.

Square up this rectangular frame and then, beginning at one end, center the 9¼" pieces on top evenly spaced about ½" apart. Drill two pilot holes through each crosspiece where it meets the long sides, and nail in place with 1" paneling nails.

Now, drill four ¹⁄₁₆" pilot holes, one at each outside corner of the bottom frame, 1" in from the ends, on the long side. The legs will go here.

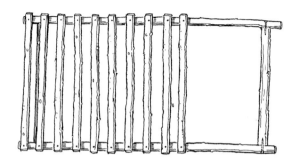

Notes on Pilot Holes

- For pilot holes that do not extend clear through a piece, remember to drill them slightly deeper than the nail will go. This will make it easier to tighten joints after the willow dries.

- Drill all pilot holes for this project with a ¹⁄₁₆" bit.

2. Attaching the Legs and Rails

Each 12" piece will function as a leg. Measure in 4" from one end of each, and drill a pilot hole; this will be the lower end of the leg. Now, rotate each leg 90 degrees and, measuring from the lower end, drill pilot holes in the *side* of each leg at 6¼", 8½", and 10¾" (the end pieces will be attached here in step 4). Then drill a pilot hole in the center of the top end of each leg.

The two 18" pieces will form the top rails. Measure in 1" from each end of the pieces and drill pilot holes through the rails. Nail the rails to the top of the leg pieces with 1⅝" paneling nails. With the pilot holes for the end pieces facing the ends, nail the legs to the bottom frame through the four holes you drilled in the lower legs. (The leg holes should line up with the corner pilot holes you previously drilled in the bottom frame.) Square up the frame.

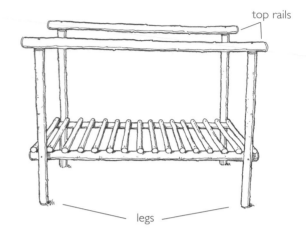

3. Assembling the Side Frames

Mark sites for pilot holes at opposite ends of each side frame piece, checking to ensure that the holes will line up with the center of the appropriate leg. The bottom-most piece on each side will also need two pilot holes for nailing to the bottom frames.

Drill pilot holes and nail the bottom-most side frame pieces to the bottom frame and the *inside* of the legs with 1⅝" paneling nails. Now, drill pilot holes through the remaining 17½" pieces and nail them to the inside of the legs with 1" paneling nails, beginning at the top of one side and evenly spacing the pieces about ½" apart. Then complete the opposite side. Trim the ends of the side frame pieces even with the outside edge of the legs.

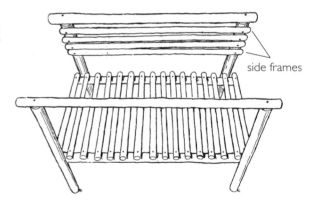

4. Attaching the End Pieces

Round the edges of the six end pieces with a rasp or Surform plane.

Measure in ⅞" from both ends of each piece and drill pilot holes through the willow. Nail three end pieces across the outside of the legs at one end of the rack with 1⅝" paneling nails, meeting the pilot holes you drilled in the side of the legs in step 2. Nail the other three end pieces across the outside of the other legs.

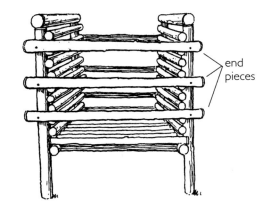

end pieces

5. Attaching the Handle

Square up the ends of the frame. Then mark the center point of all six end pieces and the two end pieces of the bottom frame. Drill pilot holes.

Measure in 1½" from the thickest end of the handle (48" flexible bender) and drill a pilot hole through the wood. Now, nail this end of the handle to the outside of the bottom frame with a 1⅝" paneling nail. Center the handle over the hole you drilled in one of the two top end pieces. Using this hole for a guide, drill through the handle, and then nail the handle with a 1⅝" paneling nail. Repeat this process for the other two end pieces, then trim off the nails.

Measure in 1½" from the other end of the handle and drill a pilot hole all the way through. Then bend the handle to the other side of the rack and nail it to the outside of the bottom frame. Again, center the handle over the hole you drilled in the top end piece. As before, drill through the handle, nail it to the top end piece with a 1⅝" nail, repeat for the other two end pieces, and trim off the nails.

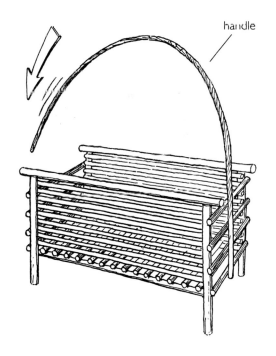

handle

Plant Stand

This plant stand found a place in the corner of our guest bathroom. I keep a basket of potpourri in the top and store an extra roll of toilet tissue on the bottom shelf. We'll have to make another one for the plant!

Preparing the Willow

Round the edges of all these pieces with a rasp or Surform plane before you begin working with them.

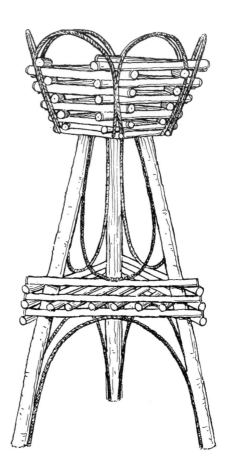

Materials				
Part	Quantity	Diameter	Length	Type of Wood
legs	3	1¼"	29"	seasoned
Bottom shelf				
side rails	9	¾"	16"	seasoned
cross rails	6	½"	cut to fit	seasoned
Basket				
edge trim	6	½"	7"	seasoned
	6	½"	cut to fit	seasoned
first row	3	¾"	8½"	seasoned
second row	3	¾"	9"	seasoned
third row	3	¾"	9½"	seasoned
fourth row	3	¾"	10"	seasoned
fifth row	3	¾"	10½"	seasoned
sixth row	3	¼"	11"	seasoned
seventh row	3	¾"	11½"	seasoned
eighth row	3	¾"	12"	seasoned
Trim				
bottom trim	3	¼"	32"	flexible bender
middle trim	3	¼"	32"	flexible bender
top trim	6	¼"	24"	flexible bender

hexagon top: 1 piece of ¾" plywood, 11" × 11"

plywood jig: 1 piece of ¼" (or thicker) plywood, 24" × 24"

paint: 1 spray can of dark brown flat enamel

I. Cutting Out the Hexagon Top

Draw two straight lines from corner to corner diagonally on the 11" × 11" piece of plywood to find the center. Choose a piece of scrap material about 7" long, measure in 5" from one end, and drive a nail through the scrap piece at this spot. Center the protruding nail point on the center of the plywood and drive it in just enough to allow the scrap piece to spin around on the nail. Hold a pencil against the 5" end, with the lead just touching the plywood top, and rotate the scrap piece, drawing a circle on the plywood as you turn. Remove the scrap piece and discard it.

Cut out the plywood circle with a jigsaw. Then, lay the plywood circle on edge on a yardstick (or tape measure) and mark the circle exactly where it rests on 0". Roll the plywood along the yard stick until it reaches the 5¼" mark. Mark this location. Continue rolling the circle along the yard stick, making marks every 5¼". You should end up with six marks — the points of a hexagon. Draw straight lines between points to form the sides of this hexagon. Cut along the lines from point to point.

To find the leg locations, draw a straight line across the hexagon top from point to point. Then, measure in 2" from a point along one of these lines and make a mark. Make a mark 2" in on every other line. Drill ⅛" pilot holes through the plywood on the 2" marks.

Paint the hexagon top dark brown. Be sure to paint the edges as well.

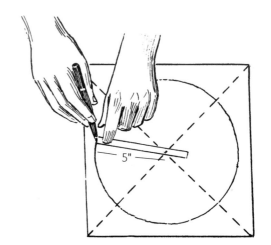

2. Preparing the Plywood Jig

Draw a straight line from corner to corner diagonally on the 24" × 24" piece of plywood to find the center. Choose a piece of scrap material about 13" long and make a mark 11" from one end. Drive a nail through the scrap piece on the mark. Center the protruding nail point on the center of the plywood and drive it in just enough to allow the scrap piece to spin around on the nail. Hold a pencil against the 11" end of the scrap piece and draw a circle on the plywood. Remove the scrap piece and discard it.

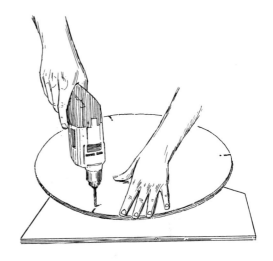

Cut out the plywood circle with a jigsaw. Then, lay the plywood circle on edge on a yard stick (or tape measure); make a mark where it rests on the 0" mark. Roll the plywood circle along the yard stick until the edge hits 23". Mark this location on the top of the plywood. Continue rolling the circle along the yard stick, making marks every 23". You should end up with three of them.

Measure in 1" from the edge at each of the three marks and drill a ⅛" pilot hole through the plywood.

3. Attaching the Legs to the Jig

Drill a ⅛" pilot hole in the center of each end of the three leg pieces. Nail the legs to the plywood jig, through the jig holes you drilled in step 2, with 8d nails.

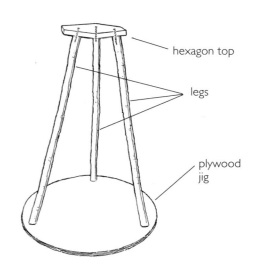

hexagon top

legs

plywood jig

Set the jig on a flat surface with the legs sticking up. Pull each leg in toward the center. Now lay the hexagon top on top of the legs and nail it to the legs with 16d nails.

Examine the plant stand from all sides to make sure it looks straight up and down and uniform from side to side. Make any adjustments you need to.

4. Attaching the Bottom Side Rails

Measure up on each leg 12" and make a mark on the outside of the legs. Center a side rail with the *top* edge even with the mark on the legs. Drill 1/16" pilot holes and nail the rail in place with 1 5/8" paneling nails. Moving around the planter, place the second side rail with the *bottom* edge even with the mark on the legs. Again, drill and nail. Place the third side rail so that one end overlaps the first rail, while the other end touches the bottom edge of the second rail. Attach as you did the other rails.

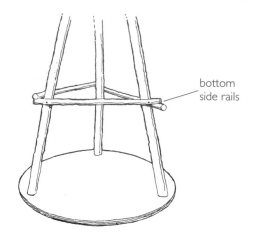

bottom side rails

5. Attaching the Bottom Cross Rails

Space the six bottom cross rail pieces evenly across the second and third bottom side rails. Drill 1/16" pilot holes through the wood and nail them to the side rails with 1" paneling nails. Trim the bottom cross rails even with the outside edge of the side rails.

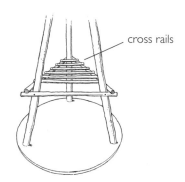

cross rails

6. Attaching the Side Rails

Place the remaining six side rails log-cabin style around the planter. Place the first one above the lowest bottom side rail, and build up from there, so that each rail rests on the ends of two lower rails. Drill 1/16" pilot holes through the wood and attach with 1 5/8" paneling nails.

7. Adding the Edge Trim

Drill two ¹⁄₁₆" pilot holes and nail a 7" edge trim piece to the *bottom* half of the plywood edge on every other side of the hexagon, using 1⅝" paneling nails. Center the other three 7" edge trim pieces on the remaining hexagon faces with the ends on top of the first three pieces (log-cabin style). Drill two ¹⁄₁₆" pilot holes in each and nail them into the top half of the plywood edge. Cut six edge trim pieces to fit in the gaps on the plywood edge. As before, drill and nail these pieces into place.

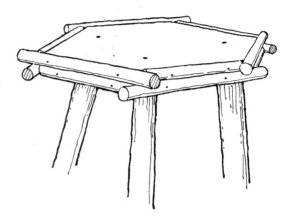

8. Assembling the Basket

This basket is bigger at the top, so each succeeding row is longer and must be nailed farther from the center of the basket. Starting with the first (bottom) row, drill ¹⁄₁₆" pilot holes and, using 1⅝" paneling nails, nail a piece on *every other* edge of the hexagon top to continue the log cabin design of the edge trim.

Lay the remaining seven rows evenly spaced in log-cabin style, drill pilot holes, and nail them in place. Place each row farther from the center to make the basket bigger at the top. Line up the inside edge of the piece you are nailing on with the outside edge of the parallel piece underneath it.

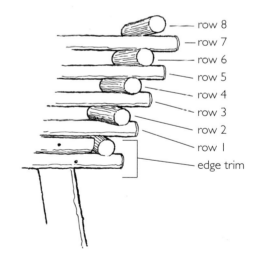

row 8
row 7
row 6
row 5
row 4
row 3
row 2
row 1
edge trim

9. Adding Bottom Trim

Drill a ¹⁄₁₆" pilot hole 1" from one end of a 32" flexible bender. Using a 1" paneling nail, nail the bender to the bottom inside edge of one leg. Extend the bender up the leg, drill another pilot hole 4½" from the bottom, and nail it in place. Bend the flexible piece so that it meets a side rail on the bottom shelf; drill and nail. Attach the bender to the inside of the opposite leg at 4½" and 1" from the bottom. Trim the bender even with the bottom of the leg.

Repeat this process, placing a bottom trim piece on the other two sides of the planter.

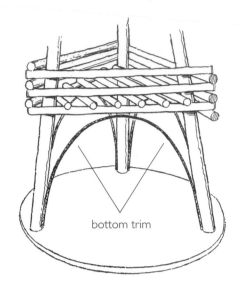

bottom trim

10. Adding Middle Trim

Drill a ¹⁄₁₆" pilot hole 1" from one end of another 32" flexible bender. Using a 1" paneling nail, nail the bender to the top inside edge of one leg. Extend the bender down the leg, drill another pilot hole 4½" from the top, and nail it in place. Bend the piece to meet the center of a top side rail on the bottom shelf; drill and nail. Attach the bender to the inside of the opposite leg at 4½" and 1" from the top. Trim off the excess length.

Repeat this process, placing a middle trim piece on the other two sides of the planter.

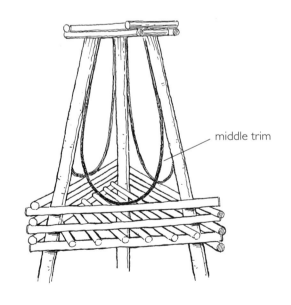

middle trim

I I. Adding Top Trim

Place the butt end of a 24" flexible bender flush with the bottom edge of the basket's edge trim. Drill a $\frac{1}{16}$" pilot hole and nail one end to the edge trim with a 1" paneling nail. Arc the bender into a horseshoe, drill a second pilot hole, and nail the other end to the edge trim. Drill two more pilot holes where the bender crosses the top row of the basket. Nail it in place.

Repeat this process, nailing a 24" top trim piece on each face of the hexagon around the planter. Be sure you nail all six benders to the top (eighth) row of the basket.

Remove the plant stand from the plywood jig.

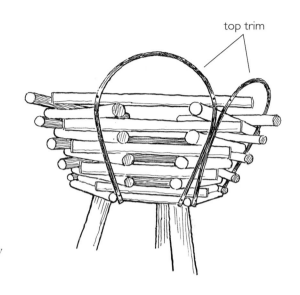

top trim

Small Hanging Basket

Mother claimed this basket the minute she saw it. She uses it in her bathroom to hold washcloths. We will have to build another one soon since I'm envisioning it in the kitchen, hung on the wall as a perfect place to display my collection of old, blue, wire-handled quart jars.

Preparing the Willow

Before you begin assembly, round the edges of all the willow pieces for this project with a rasp or Surform plane.

Materials				
Part	Quantity	Diameter	Length	Type of Wood
log cabin box	8	½"	6"	seasoned
	11	½"	12"	seasoned
Arches				
inner back arch	1	¼"	24"	flexible bender
outer back arch	1	¼"	32"	flexible bender
front arch	1	¼"	32"	flexible bender
Support Braces				
back brace	1	½"	cut to fit	seasoned
side braces	4	½"	3"	seasoned
top trim	9	¼"	6½"	seasoned

1. Assembling the Bottom

To build the bottom of the log cabin box, lay one of the 6" box pieces on a flat surface. Evenly space five of the 12" pieces across the 6" piece, with 1" of each extending beyond the shorter piece. Drill $1/16$" pilot holes through the 12" pieces where they overlap the 6" piece and nail in place with 1" paneling nails. Place another 6" piece underneath the opposite ends of the crosspieces, making sure the pieces are straight and evenly spaced. Drill a second set of pilot holes, and nail.

Note on Pilot Holes and Nails

- Drill all pilot holes for this project with a $1/16$" bit.

- Use 1" paneling nails for this project, *unless otherwise specified*.

2. Building the Log-Cabin Style Box

To begin building up the front, back, and sides of your box, place two more 6" side pieces parallel to the bottom ones, sandwiching the 12" pieces. Drill pilot holes 1" in from the ends, and nail the side piece to the outermost cross piece.

Continue to build log-cabin style, placing two 12" pieces along the front and back, perpendicular to the side pieces. Drill and nail as before.

Continue to alternate and attach 6" and 12" pieces to complete the box, checking it each level to be sure the four sides are straight and square.

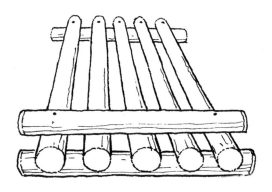

3. Forming the Back Arches

Decide which long side of the box you want to use for the back of your hanging basket. To form the inner back arch, position one end of the 24" flexible bender against the back about 3" in from the side, with the bottom of the arch piece flush with the bottom of the box. Drill pilot holes where the bender touches the back pieces and nail it in place. Bend the piece around, forming a nice arch and placing the other end 3" in from the opposite side. Drill and nail.

To form the outer back arch, place one end of one of the 32" flexible benders at an outside back corner of your log-cabin style box, right where the rungs meet and overlap, keeping the bottom end even with the basket bottom. Drill four pilot holes and nail the bender to the back rungs. Shape the piece into an arch and bend it down to the other outside back corner. Drill and nail as you did the first side.

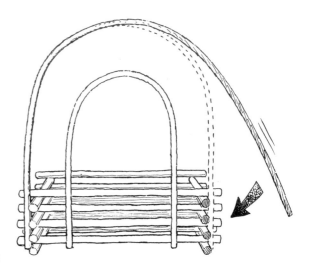

4. Forming the Front Arch

Turn your log-cabin style box onto one side. Place the remaining 32" flexible bender parallel to the outer back arch but in front of the back rungs. Drill pilot holes where the bender intersects the rungs, and nail in place. Lay the basket on its other side. Bend the second bender around, matching the arc of the outer back arch; drill four more pilot holes and nail it on the opposite side of the baskets. Be sure both ends of the bender are even with the bottom rung.

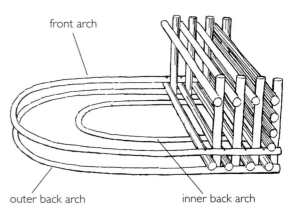

front arch

outer back arch   inner back arch

5. Attaching the Back Brace

From the back of the hanging basket, measure the distance across the inside of the outer back arch, at the top of the inner arch. Cut a ½" diameter back brace to fit here.

Drill pilot holes into the ends of the brace and also through the outer back arch, where the arch and brace meet. Nail this brace with 1⅝" *paneling nails* to the outer back arch so it rests against the inner arch. Do *not* nail the inner arch to this brace.

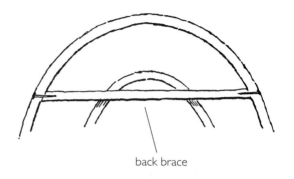

back brace

6. Attaching the Side Braces

Insert the 3" side brace pieces, two on each side, between the front arch and the outer back arch. Position them 2" and 4" from the top rung of the log-cabin style box. Use these pieces to adjust the space between the inner arch and the front and back arches. Drill pilot holes into one end of each side brace (the end that will abut the inner back arch), and also through the diameter of each side brace where it will be nailed to the outer bark arch and the front arch. Drill four corresponding pilot holes through the sides of the inner back arch and four through the front arch. Nail these side braces to the front and back arches and to the inner arch.

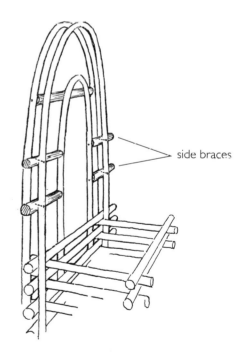

side braces

7. Attaching Top Trim

Insert one of the 6½" trim pieces at the top of and between the front and outer back arches. Slip the lower end *behind* the inner arch and *in front of* the back brace.

Drill a pilot hole ¾" from the end and nail this piece to the back brace. Make sure the piece stands straight, then drill pilot holes where it meets the inner back arch and the peak of the bigger arches. Nail it in place from the front.

Similarly, insert, adjust, and nail the remaining 6½" pieces, four on each side of the center trim piece. The bottoms of these pieces should all come together just below the inner back arch, and fan out above upper arches.

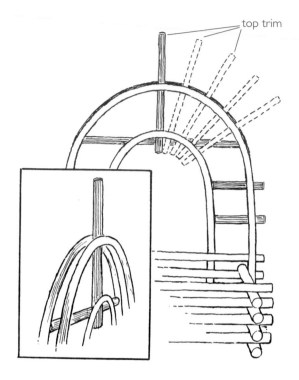

top trim

Large Hanging Basket

Who ever has enough baskets? I could use several more of these. I use one in the kitchen to hold tin foil, wax paper, and paper towels. I use another one in the guest bath to hold extra toilet tissue. Still other large hanging baskets line our porch in the summer, filled with flowering begonias and geraniums.

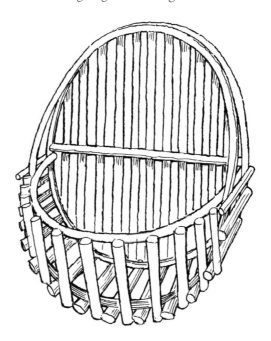

Materials				
Part	Quantity	Diameter	Length	Type of Wood
hoops	2	½"	72"	flexible bender
back rails	11	¾"	18"	seasoned
back support	1	¾"	cut to fit	seasoned
rim bender	1	½"	28"	flexible bender
front/bottom rails	27	½" to ¾"	9"	seasoned
template: 1 piece of ¾" plywood, 20" × 20"				
floral wire: 6 pieces of floral wire 6" long				

I. Preparing the Template

Draw a straight line from corner to corner diagonally on the 20" × 20" piece of plywood to find the center. Choose a piece of scrap material 10" to 12" long and make a mark 8" from one end. Drive a nail through the scrap piece on the mark. Hammer the protruding nail point to the center of the plywood template, driving it in just enough to allow the scrap piece to spin around on the nail. Hold a pencil against the 8" end of the scrap piece and draw a circle on the template. Remove the scrap piece and discard it.

Drive 6d nails along the circle about 3" to 4" apart. Drive them in deep enough to hold the hoop benders on the inside of the circle.

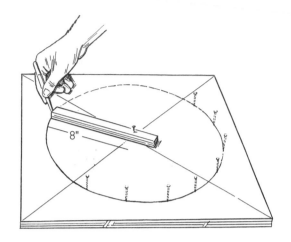

2. Assembling the Hoops

Make a mark 6" in from the *thicker* end of the two hoop benders. Now, using a metal straight edge and utility knife, cut through the benders diagonally from the mark all the way to the tip of the thick end.

Beginning with the trimmed end, place one of the benders inside the nails on the template. When you complete the circle, loop the remainder of the bender on top of the trimmed end and mark the diagonal cut you need to splice the two pieces together. Remove the bender from the template, cut along the diagonal as you did before, return the bender to the template, and check the fit of the spliced joint. Trim or whittle as needed to make a good fit. Repeat this process to make the second hoop.

floral wire

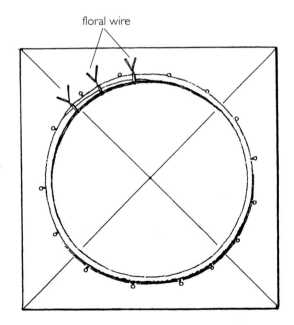

Now, slip a piece of floral wire under each bender at the center of the spliced joint. Keeping the joint aligned and tight, make at least two wraps around the joint and twist the ends of the wire together. Trim off the excess wire. Place another wire wrap about ¾" from each end of the joint. Let the hoops season in the template for 3 days.

3. Attaching the Back Rails

Mark one of the back rail pieces ¾" from the end. Pick one of the hoops for the back and place it on top of this back rail piece, with the outside edge of the spliced joint on the mark. (This will be the *bottom* of the hoop.) Position the back rail piece straight across the diameter of the back hoop. Drill ¹⁄₁₆" pilot holes through the hoop and nail it with 1" or 1⅝" paneling nails to the back rail. The spliced joint will be placed at the bottom of the back hoop.

Trim the excess back rail even with the top of the hoop. Now, place another back rail piece beside the center one, ¾" away and with ¾" protruding at the bottom. Drill, nail, and trim as you did for the first one.

Alternating sides, repeat this process adding back rails until there are two on each side of the center rail. Beginning with the third rail from the center, the remaining back rails should be nailed so that the bottom ends meet but do not extend beyond the outer edge of the back hoop. Trim them all at the top, as you did the others.

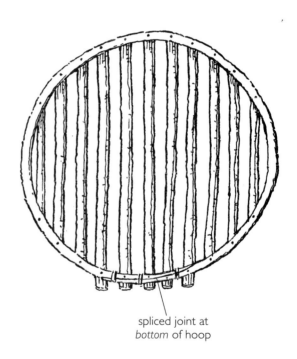

spliced joint at *bottom* of hoop

Note on Pilot Holes

Drill all pilot holes for this project with a ¹⁄₁₆" bit.

4. Attaching the Back Support

Cut the ¾" back support piece to fit across the *inside* diameter of the hoop, perpendicular to and on top of the back rails. Drill pilot holes and nail to the support every other back rail with 1⅝" paneling nails.

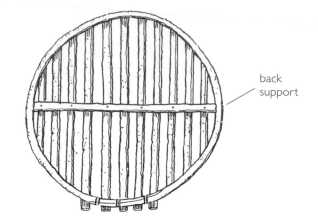

back support

5. Attaching the Front Hoop and Rim Bender

Keeping the spliced joints at what will be the basket's bottom, place the front hoop on top of the back hoop. Drill pilot holes and nail the front hoop to the back hoop at the top through the three center back rails using 1⅝" paneling nails.

Put one end of the trim bender under the back support piece against the inside of the back hoop. Drill a pilot hole and nail it to the back support with a 1⅝" paneling nail. Arc the bender across the back of the basket. Drill a second pilot hole and nail the rim bender to this side of the back support piece, too.

Measure 3½" from the back hoop along the rim bender on each side. Mark these locations. Make sure the rim bender is perpendicular to the back hoop. Then pull the front hoop away from the back hoop and center it on the 3½" marks. Drill pilot holes through the front hoop and nail it to the rim bender with 1" paneling nails.

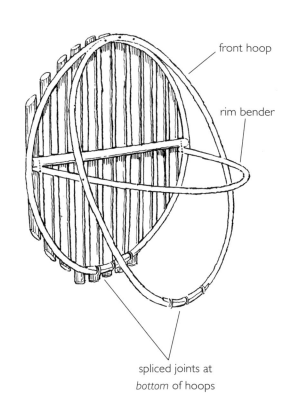

front hoop

rim bender

spliced joints at *bottom* of hoops

6. Attaching the Front and Bottom Rails

Place the first bottom rail at the center bottom of the basket, outside the hoops and with ¾" protruding beyond the front hoop. Make sure this piece is square with the back. Drill pilot holes in the rail and nail it to the back and front hoops with 1" or 1⅝" paneling nails.

Place a front rail against the first bottom rail. Make sure it is straight, then drill pilot holes and nail it to the first bottom rail (*not* the front hoop) and the rim bender with 1" or 1⅝" paneling nails.

Alternating a bottom and then a front rail, drill pilot holes and nail the rest of the rails in place until the curved bottom reaches the rim and the front rails approach the point where the front hoop and the rim meet. Trim the front rails ¼" past the top edge of the rim bender. Trim the bottom rails even with the outside edge of the front rails. (The finished rails will be progressively shorter as the bottom curves upward and the front curves back.)

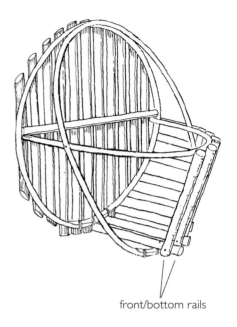

front/bottom rails

Trimming and Finishing

If you measure each bottom and front rail carefully, you can cut them to the proper length before drilling and nailing them in place.

Complete the basket with one of the finishes described in chapter 5, or leave it natural, as you wish.

Children's Table

One of the greatest joys of being grandparents is that we get to play with toys again! This table and the children's chair (the next project) were the most fun to build. We had lots of help from our five-year-old grandson.

Materials				
Part	Quantity	Diameter	Length	Type of Wood
legs	4	1½"	16"	seasoned
top rungs	2	1¾"	16"	seasoned
top supports	2	1¾"	24"	seasoned
cross supports	2	1"	cut to fit	seasoned
center support	1	1½"	cut to fit	seasoned
table top	approx. 35	¾"	24"	flexible bender
trim	8	½"	50"	flexible bender
guide piece: 1 piece of thin scrap wood, 24" long and 1–2" wide				

1. Building the Basic Frame

Drill ⅛" pilot holes in the center of (a) the top of the four leg pieces and (b) each end of the two top rung pieces.

Mark in line and drill a ⅛" pilot hole 3" from each end of both 24" top supports. Then nail the top supports to the tops of the legs with 16d nails. Now, drill ⅛" in-line pilot holes through the *sides* of the top supports, 3¼" from each end. Position the top rungs between the top supports and nail them in place through these pilot holes.

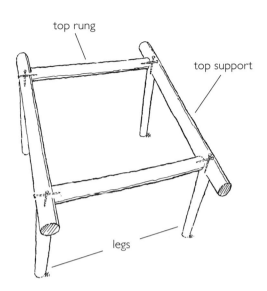

top rung

top support

legs

2. Attaching Cross and Center Supports

Turn the table frame upside down, square it up, and make sure the legs are straight. Measure from the inside of one leg diagonally across to the opposite leg. Cut a cross support to fit here. Do the same for the other pair of legs and cross support. Drill ⅛" pilot holes in the center of each end of the cross support, and another in the middle of each cross support.

Drill a ⅛" pilot hole 4" up from the bottom of one leg and another 4" up from the bottom of the leg that is diagonally across from it. Make sure the pilot holes line up along the diagonal. Nail one of the cross supports between these two legs with 16d nails.

Drill diagonally facing ³⁄₃₂" pilot holes in the other two legs 5" up from the bottom of each. Nail the other cross support between these legs. Now, nail the two cross supports together in the center with a 6d nail.

Measure between the top rungs at the inside center and cut the center support piece to fit. Drill a ⅛" pilot hole through the top rungs into the end of the center support and nail the latter in place with 16d nails.

Set the table right side up on a flat surface and make sure it is squared.

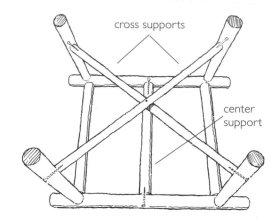

3. Preparing the Table Top

Round the edges of all the table top pieces with a file or Surform plane or rasp before you nail them to the top.

Using 1⅝" paneling nails, fasten the first piece slightly overhanging the end of, and centered on, the top supports. Similarly position and nail the second piece on the other end of the table. Now, lightly *tack* a straight piece of scrap wood to the ends of these pieces for a guide in completing the table top.

Continue placing pieces on the top with one end against the guide. Start at the ends and work toward the middle. *Stagger the nails so you won't split the top support pieces.* Before you nail the last four top pieces, lay them in place and see if they will cover the space sufficiently. If not, choose different diameter pieces until you get the correct coverage, then nail them in place.

4. Trimming and Tightening

Turn the table upside down on a flat surface. Drill a
$\frac{1}{16}$" pilot hole through the *center* of an inside trim
piece and nail it with 1" or $1\frac{5}{8}$" paneling nails to
the middle of a top support on the underneath side.
Bend the trim piece in front of the cross supports,
drill two $\frac{1}{16}$" pilot holes, and nail the trim to the
legs on each side, maintaining a nice arched shape.
Cut the trim even with the bottom of the legs.
Repeat this process around the table, nailing the
center of the other three inside trim pieces to the
other top support and the top rungs.

Drill a $\frac{1}{16}$" pilot hole and nail the center of an
outside trim piece to the middle of a top support
on the outside center. Bend the trim to the outside
corner of a leg. Drill two $\frac{1}{16}$" pilot holes and nail
the trim to the legs with 1" or $1\frac{5}{8}$" paneling nails.
Trim off the excess length at the bottom. Repeat
this process around the table, as you did with the
inside trim.

Set the table upright on a sturdy flat surface and
check it for stability. If it wobbles, adjust the legs
by trimming off *small* amounts until it is stable.

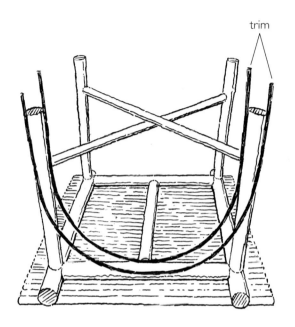

trim

Children's Chair

The design for these chairs was inspired by the old ladder-back chairs we use in our kitchen. It's a simple, sturdy, and functional design that has been used for centuries. The dimensions are based on our two-year-old and five-year-old grandchildren. Notice we had to build *two* chairs!

Materials				
Part	Quantity	Diameter	Length	Type of Wood
back legs	2	1½"	20" (straight)	seasoned
bottom back rungs	2	1½"	10"	seasoned
top back rungs	3	1"	10"	seasoned
side rungs	4	1½"	10"	seasoned
front legs	2	1½"	9"	seasoned
front rungs	2	1½"	12"	seasoned
front trim	1	¾"	13½"	seasoned
seat rails	approx. 13	½"	approx. 13"	seasoned

1. Preparing the Back Legs

Lay the back legs next to each other on a flat surface with the thick (bottom) end toward you. Hold them together and look at the way they fit against each other. Roll one of the legs against the other until you get the tightest fit from top to bottom. Through the center of each back leg, drill two ⅛" in-line holes, one 4" from the bottom and the other 7½" from the bottom. Mark these pieces L (left) and R (right) at the top hole. (You can cover or erase these marks later.) You will attach the side rungs here in step 2.

Rotate the back legs 90 degrees so that the holes you drilled are on the side. On what is now the upward side, measure up from the bottom of each back leg and mark these locations: 3¾", 7¼", 10½", 13½", and 16½". Drill ⅛" pilot holes in line with each other in the center of the limb on these marks. You will attach the back rungs here in step 2.

Rotate the back legs until the L and R marks touch each other. Start 16d nails through the series of five holes you just drilled in each back leg. Drive the nails through the limb until they slightly stick out on the other side.

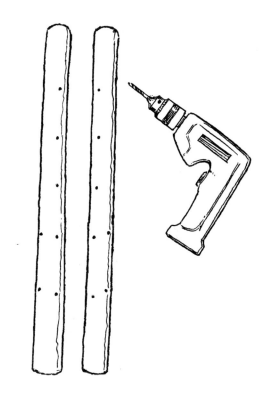

2. Attaching the Back and Side Rungs

Drill a ⅛" pilot hole in the center of both ends of all five back rung pieces (drill these holes about 2" deep). Starting at the bottom, nail the two (1½") bottom back rungs to the back legs with 16d nails. Continuing up the legs, nail the three top back rungs to the back legs with 16d nails. You may have to trim some of the rung pieces to get a good fit.

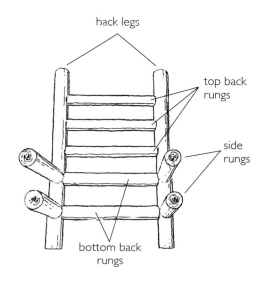

back legs

top back rungs

side rungs

bottom back rungs

Drill a ⅛" pilot hole in both ends of the side rung pieces. Place the side rungs on the back leg holes you marked R and L, and then nail them in place with 16d nails.

3. Attaching the Front Legs and Front Rungs

Through the center of each front leg drill two ⅛" pilot holes, one 4" from the bottom and the other 7½" from the bottom. Mark an × on the top holes with a felt tip marker.

Rotate the front legs 90 degrees so that the holes are on the side. On what is now the upward side, measure up from the bottom and mark at 3¾" and 7¼". Drill ⅛" pilot holes in line with each other through the center of the limb on these marks. (You will shortly attach the front rungs here.)

Rotate the front legs until the × marks touch each other. Start 16d nails through the two holes you just drilled at the 3¾" and 7¼" marks. Drive the nails through the limb until they stick out slightly on the other side.

Drill a ⅛" pilot hole in the center of both ends of the front rung pieces. Then, nail the front rungs between the two front legs using 16d nails.

Fit the front leg section to the front ends of the side rungs with the × marks against the ends of the top side rung. Nail them together with 16d nails.

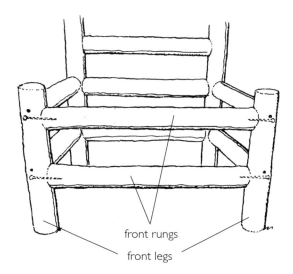

front rungs

front legs

4. Attaching Front Trim and Seat Rails

Center the front trim piece between the front legs with the top edge about ½" above the top edge of the top front rung. Drill a ¹⁄₁₆" pilot hole angled down through the center of the front trim piece into the top front rung. Nail with a 1⅝" paneling nail.

Adjust the trim piece across the front rung, and then drill ¹⁄₁₆" pilot holes through the trim and angled into the front of both front legs. Nail with 1⅝" paneling nails.

Set the chair on a flat surface and adjust the frame until it does not tip. Check to make sure the front legs are square with the back legs. Adjust them as necessary.

Place the first seat rail in the center of the seat section. Butt it against the front trim piece. Drill ¹⁄₁₆" pilot holes through the center of the trim and into the top center of both the top front rung and parallel back rung. Nail the trim in place with 1⅝" paneling nails.

Now, space the next seat rail about ½" from the first, drill as before, and nail it in place. Continue in this manner in both directions across the seat. *Alternate thick and thin seat rail ends to keep the spacing fairly even.* The chair is 2" wider in the front, so the spaces between the seat rails will be slightly wider at the front.

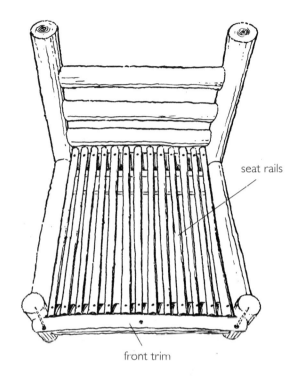

seat rails

front trim

Reminder on Trimming and Tightening

As with all bent willow furniture, cut off and file down any nail tips that stick out too far, and smooth the rough edges. Let willow furniture season for 3 to 6 weeks out of direct sunlight. Examine your chair in 3 to 6 months and drive in any nails that may have popped out as the wood dried.

# CHAPTER 4

# More Advanced Projects

Unlike milled lumber, willow is rarely uniform in dimension. The only constant is the center line of each piece. Use the center line as a reference point when building these advanced projects. Develop an eye for form and place the natural curves of the piece to benefit the design.

Don't be afraid to design your own pieces. If you see an old table or chair (or any other piece) you would like to reproduce with willow, study the

Tools and Hardware for Projects in This Chapter

- Chisel
- Deck screws: 2", 3"
- Dikes or side-cutting pliers
- Drill with bits: $\frac{1}{16}$", $\frac{3}{32}$", $\frac{1}{8}$", $\frac{3}{16}$", $\frac{1}{4}$", $\frac{5}{16}$", $\frac{3}{8}$", $\frac{1}{2}$", plus $\frac{1}{2}$" and $\frac{3}{4}$" spade or paddle bits
- Electric sabre or hand key hole saw
- Flat double-cut file
- Hacksaw
- Hammer
- Level
- Marker (felt-tip, chalk, or pencil)

- Nails: 6d, 16d
- Nail set
- Paneling nails: 1", $1\frac{5}{8}$"
- Pliers
- Protractor
- Pruning or bow saw
- Pruning shears
- Rasp or Surform plane
- Saber saw
- Safety glasses and gloves
- Socket wrench
- Tape measure
- Utility knife

basic structure. Look carefully at the joints and the support pieces. Then build a small model out of willow twigs. It really helps to see your ideas in three-dimensions, and you can easily modify a small model.

You can complete any of the projects in this chapter with one of the finishes described in chapter 5, or leave it natural, as you wish.

A traditional bent willow chair design (instructions begin on page 64).

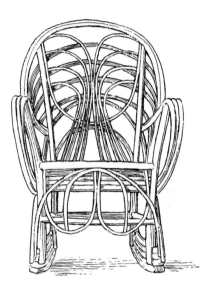

A variation of the traditional design crafted for use as a rocking chair.

Gypsy Willow Chair

This is a very common willow design. Joe Elders, who had built this design for sixty-four years before he showed it to me, called it a gypsy design. Gypsies built this furniture for their own use as they traveled and sometimes built extra pieces to sell along the way. My grandpa called it "stick furniture." I loved it then — and it's still my favorite design. We use these chairs indoors and outdoors.

Notes on Materials

❦ Your two 23" limbs for the back legs should curve slightly in toward the top. Otherwise, you will need to lengthen the bottom back rung by 1" to compensate.

❦ The 18" limb for the front bottom rung should be at least 1¾" in diameter, but can be a bit thicker. You need a sturdy limb because the arm benders will be nailed to it.

❦ The 26" limb for the front top rung is longer than the bottom rung to support the arm benders and the seat rails. This piece tends to split, so be sure you use a sturdy limb.

Materials				
Part	Quantity	Diameter	Length	Type of Wood
back legs	2	1¾"	23", slightly curved at the top	seasoned
back rungs	2	1¾"	18", (one 19" if the back legs do not curve)	seasoned
side rungs	4	1¾"	18"	seasoned
front legs	2	1¾"	14"	seasoned
front bottom rung	1	1¾"	18"	seasoned
front top rung	1	1¾"	26"	seasoned
seat brace	1	1¾"	cut to fit	seasoned
side braces	4	1¾"	cut to fit	seasoned
slanted braces	2	1¾"	cut to fit	seasoned
back support	1	1¾"	28"	seasoned
seat support	1	1¾"	17"	seasoned
arm benders	8	¾"	67"	flexible bender
back benders	4	¾"	67"	flexible bender
seat/back rails	25–30	¾"	cut to fit	flexible bender
back trim	1	¾"	32"	flexible bender

template: 1 piece of ¾" plywood, about 28" × 28", cut to fit

clamps: 2 3" or 4" clamps

I. Preparing the Back Legs

Lay the back leg pieces on a flat surface so that the top ends curve slightly toward each other. Drill two ⅛" pilot holes through the front of both back legs, one 9" from the top and the other 7" from the bottom. (This is where you will soon attach the side rungs.)

Rotate the legs 90 degrees so that the holes are on the side. Drill two more pilot holes slightly underneath the level of the first holes.

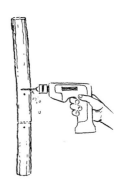

2. Attaching the Back and Side Rungs

Drill a pilot hole in the center of both ends of the two back rungs. (Remember, if the back leg limbs do not curve, lengthen the bottom back rung.) As always, drill these holes a bit deeper than the nail will go. Then nail the back rungs to the back legs with 16d nails. *The top rung must be a straight piece.*

Drill a pilot hole in the center of both ends of the two side rungs. Then nail the side rungs to the back leg section with 16d nails.

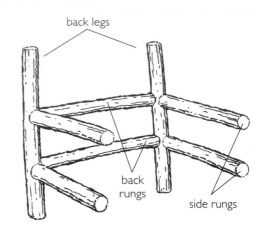

Note on Pilot Holes

Drill all pilot holes for this project with a ⅛" bit, unless otherwise specified.

3. Attaching the Front Leg Section

Drill two pilot holes through the side of both front legs, 7" from the bottom.

Drill a pilot hole in the center of both ends of the front bottom rung. Nail it to the front legs with 16d nails.

Fit the front leg section against the back leg section and drill a pilot hole in each front limb, centered on the pilot holes you already drilled in the side rungs. Fasten with 16d nails.

Now set the base on a level surface and square it so the legs rest flat on the floor.

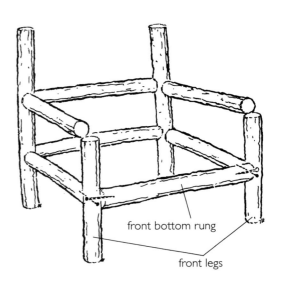

4. Attaching the Front Top Rung and Seat Brace

Center the front top rung across the front legs. Drill into the front of the rung two pilot holes centered on the side rung pilot holes. Fasten with 16d nails. (Be sure the base is sitting flat on the floor, and square the side rungs before you nail the front top rung on.) Next, drill two vertical pilot holes through the front top rung and into the ends of the legs. Fasten with 16d nails.

Set one end of a level on the front top rung and the other end on the back top rung. The frame should slope slightly toward the back to make the most comfortable seat.

Cut the seat brace to fit between the top side rungs. Position it *under* the level, parallel to and halfway between the front and back top rungs. Mark the top side rungs where the brace nails will go. Turn the base on its side and drill pilot holes through the side rungs into the brace. Fasten with 16d nails.

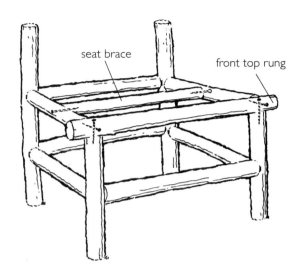

5. Attaching the Side Braces

Measure and cut the side braces to fit vertically between the chair rungs on all four sides. Drill a pilot hole in the center of both ends of each side brace. Mark and drill corresponding pilot holes through the top and bottom rungs. Fasten the four braces with 16d nails.

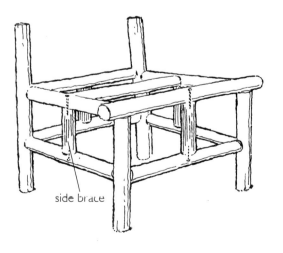

6. Attaching the Slanted Braces

Cut the slanted braces to fit diagonally between the seat brace and the bottom rung in front and back. Drill two diagonal pilot holes through the top of the seat brace into the center of the slanted brace's diagonal. Be sure to stagger the holes. Nail with 16d nails. Then drill one pilot hole through each bottom rung into the center of the slanted braces. Nail as before.

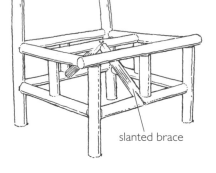

slanted brace

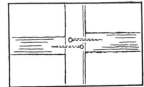

In step 6, stagger the nails in the seat brace to avoid splitting the wood.

7. Attaching the Back and Seat Supports

Center the back support across the top of the back legs. Drill pilot holes down through the support and into the legs. Fasten with 16d nails.

Drill in-line pilot holes 1½ inches in from each end and one in the center of the seat support. Position this piece in front of and level with the top back rung. Nail at the rung with 16d nails. (The seat and back rails will be nailed to this limb later.)

back support

seat support

8. Attaching the First Two Arm Benders

Drill a 1/16" pilot hole and, with a 6d nail, fasten the butt end of an arm bender to the *inside* of the front bottom rung. The bender should lean against the inside of the front leg. Wrap the arm piece up and tuck it under the back support, against the back leg. Nail the bender to the back support and trim off the extra length.

Now attach an arm bender on the other side of the chair using the same method.

9. Completing the Arms

Put three additional benders on each side. Alternate the sides to keep the frame from warping. Nail the benders to each other every 6 to 8 inches with 1" or 1⅝" paneling nails as required to maintain the contour. Remember to stagger the nails for each layer.

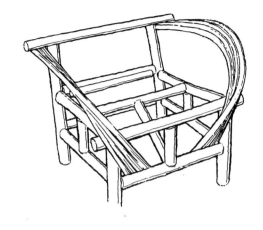

10. Preparing the template

Draw a straight line across the plywood template 4" from the bottom. Measure the distance from outside edge to outside edge of the arm benders, and mark this distance on the line drawn on the template. Trim off the excess plywood.

Now measure the width of the arm benders on each side, and mark these measurements on each end of the template line. Notch the template to fit between the arm benders. Mark the center of the line between the notches (see caption at right).

Using a scrap piece of willow about 17" long, ½" to ¾" diameter, measure 1" from one end and drive a nail through the center on this mark. Place the end of the nail on the center mark of the template line and drive it in just enough to allow the willow piece to pivot on the nail. Trim the length of the scrap piece even with the edge of the plywood at the outside edge of the arm benders.

Hold a pencil against the trimmed end of the scrap piece and mark an arch on the template. Remove the scrap piece and discard it. Cut out the template with a saw. Clamp or tack the template to the back legs.

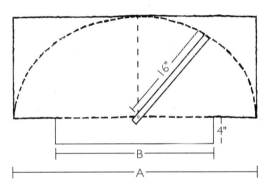

A. Distance from outer edge of left arm benders to outer edge of right arm benders.
B. Distance from inner edge of left arm benders to inner edge of right arm benders.

11. Attaching the Back Benders

Clamp the plywood template to the back legs of the chair. (See page 25 in chapter 2 for a discussion of templates.) The template will support the benders and give a nice, even shape to the back.

Drill a $\frac{1}{16}$" pilot hole and, using a 6d nail, fasten the butt end of the first bender to the inside of the top side rung. Wrap the bender outside the arm, against the back support, and around the template. Drill a $\frac{1}{16}$" pilot hole, and nail the bender to the inside of the top back rung on the other side and to the back support. Trim off the extra length. Do *not* nail the first bender to the template.

Start the next bender on the opposite side and wrap it the other way. Alternating sides will give a more even shape to the back. Nail the second bender to the first, using 1" or $1\frac{5}{8}$" paneling nails every 6 to 8 inches, as required to maintain the contour. Remember to stagger the nails to avoid splitting the wood. When all four back benders are in place (and lined up along the side rungs), remove the template.

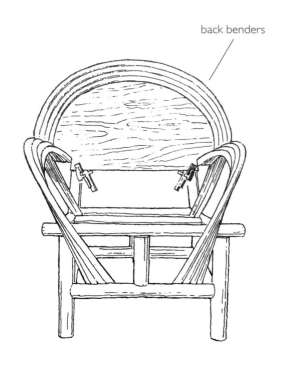

back benders

12. Assembling Seat and Back Rails

Measure the seat length from outer edge of the bottom support to the front edge of the front top rung. Cut the first seat rail, and position it in the middle of the seat. Drill $\frac{1}{16}$" pilot holes, and nail the seat rail to the seat support, seat brace, and front rung with $1\frac{5}{8}$" paneling nails.

Splicing Back Benders

You may need to splice some of the back benders to make them long enough. You can find information on splicing in chapter 2, page 26.

Now measure the center height of the back, from the base of the seat support to the top of the second back bender (measure from the *front* of the seat support to the *back* of the back bender). Cut a back rail to fit and position it next to the seat rail you just installed. Nail it with 1" or 1⅝" paneling nails to the front of the back support and to the back of the first or second back bender.

Install the rest of the back and seat rails, working from the middle out to each side. Remember to put a seat rail on, then a back rail. *Because the back is wider at the top, the back rails will fan out.* Trim off the extra length.

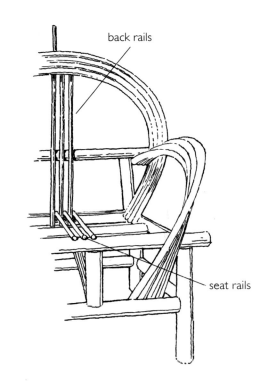

back rails

seat rails

13. Attaching Back Trim (optional)

Drill ¹⁄₁₆" pilot holes about 4" apart in the back trim piece. Using 1" or 1⅝" paneling nails, nail the back trim to the back benders on the back of the chair. This trim piece is optional. It gives the chair a more finished look.

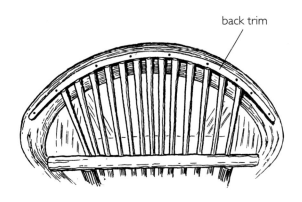

back trim

Gypsy Willow
Loveseat or Porch Swing

The dimensions of the gypsy willow chair were adapted to make this loveseat or porch swing. You can build the loveseat and modify it into a porch swing, and then use it as both if you wish. You may want to trim the legs shorter if you want only a porch swing. We did not trim the legs on ours because we use it as a swing in the summer, and then move it inside in the winter as a loveseat. (To make this loveseat into a porch swing, follow the addition to step 7 discussed on page 78.)

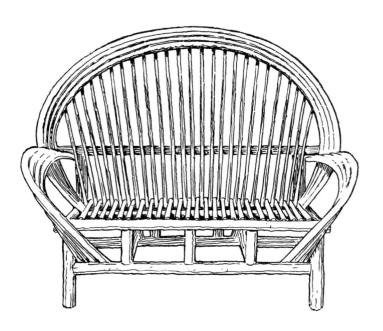

Materials

Part	Quantity	Diameter	Length	Type of Wood
back legs	2	1¾" (2½" for swing)	29", slightly curved at the top	seasoned
back rungs	2	1¾"	37" (one 38" if the back legs do not curve)	seasoned
side rungs	4	1¾"	18"	seasoned
front legs	2	1¾"	14½"	seasoned
bottom rung	1	1¾"	37"	seasoned
front top rung	1	1¾"	45"	seasoned
seat brace	1	1¾"	cut to fit	seasoned
side braces	7	1¾"	cut to fit	seasoned
slanted braces	4	1¾"	cut to fit	seasoned
back support	1	1¾"	56"	seasoned
seat support	1	1¾"	36"	seasoned
arm benders	8	¾"	75"	flexible
back benders	4	¾"	75"	flexible
seat/back rails	50–55	¾"	cut to fit	flexible
back trim	1	¾"	56"	flexible

template: 1 piece of ¾" plywood, about 48" × 24", cut to fit

clamps: 2 3" or 4" clamps

Extra Materials and Hardware for Porch Swing

front chain support	1	2½"	61"	seasoned
rear chain support	1	2½"	61"	seasoned

washers: 6 ⅜" plain washers; 4 ⅜" fender washers

bolts: 4 ⅜" × 4" eye bolts; 2 ⅜" × 5½" carriage bolts

nuts: 4 plain ⅜" nuts; 2 ⅜" lock nuts

³⁄₁₆" chain to hang the swing

Notes on Materials

❧ Your 29" limbs for the back legs should curve slightly in toward the top. Otherwise, you will need to lengthen the bottom back rung by 1" to compensate.

❧ The 37" limb for the front bottom rung should be at least 1¾" in diameter, but it can be a bit thicker. You need a sturdy limb because the arm bender will be nailed to it.

❧ The 45" limb for the front top rung is longer than the bottom rung to support the arm benders and seat rails. This piece tends to split, so be sure you use a sturdy limb.

❧ If you intend to make this piece a porch swing (see page 78), the chain support limbs must be strong, solid limbs.

I. Preparing the Back Legs

Lay the back leg pieces on a flat surface so that the top ends curve slightly toward each other. Use 1¾" limbs for a loveseat but 2½" limbs for a porch swing. Drill two ⅛" pilot holes through the front of both legs, one 14½" from the top and the other 7" from the bottom. (This is where you will soon attach the side rungs.)

Rotate the legs 90 degrees so that the holes are on the side. Drill two more pilot holes slightly underneath the level of the first holes.

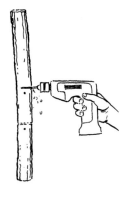

Note on Pilot Holes

Drill all *pilot* holes for this project with a ⅛" bit, unless otherwise specified. (You will also need to drill ⅜" holes for the chain support hardware if you adapt the loveseat into a porch swing.)

2. Attaching the Back and Side Rungs

Drill a pilot hole in the center of both ends of the two back rungs. (Remember, if the back leg limbs do not curve, lengthen the bottom back rung.) As always, drilll these holes a bit deeper than the nail will go. Then nail the back rungs to the back legs with 16d nails. *The top rung must be a straight piece.*

Drill a pilot hole in the center of both ends of the two side rungs. Then nail the side rungs to the back leg section with 16d nails.

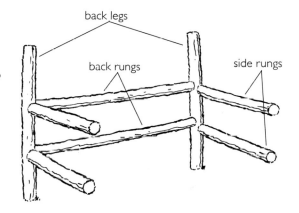

3. Attaching the Front Leg Section

Drill two pilot holes through the side of both front legs, 7" from the bottom.

Drill a pilot hole in the center of each end of the front bottom rung. Nail it to the front legs with 16d nails.

Fit the front leg section against the back leg section and drill a pilot hole in each front limb, centered on the pilot holes you already drilled in the side rungs. Fasten with 16d nails.

Now set the base on a level surface and square it so the legs sit flat on the floor.

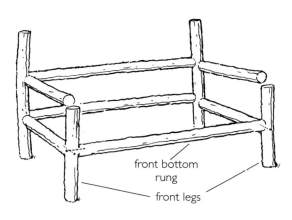

4. Attaching the Front Top Rung and Seat Brace

Center the front top rung across the front legs. Drill pilot holes into the front of the rung, centered on the side rung pilot holes. Fasten wth 16d nails. (Be sure the base is resting flat on the floor, and square the side rungs before you nail the front top rung on.) Next, drill two vertical pilot holes through the front top rung and into the ends of the legs. Fasten with 16d nails.

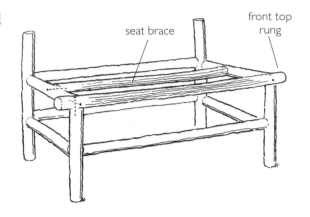

seat brace

front top rung

Set one end of a level on the front top rung and the other end on the top back rung. The frame should slope slightly toward the back to make the most comfortable seat.

Cut the seat brace to fit between the top side rungs. Position it *under* the level, parallel to and halfway between the front and back top rungs. Mark the top side rungs where the brace nails will go. Turn the base on its side and drill pilot holes through the side rungs into the brace. Fasten with 16d nails.

5. Attaching the Side Braces

Measure and cut the seven side braces to fit vertically between the rungs on all four sides. Put three braces in front, two in back, and one on each end; space the braces evenly.

Drill a pilot hole in the center of both ends of each side brace. Mark and drill corresponding pilot holes through the top and bottom rungs. Nail all seven braces in with 16d nails.

side braces

6. Attaching the Slanted Braces

Cut the four slanted braces to fit diagonally between the seat brace and the bottom rung in front and back. Space matching pairs of braces 6" from the center of the seat brace. Drill four diagonal pilot holes through the top of the seat brace into the center of the slanted braces. Be sure to stagger the holes. Nail with 16d nails. Then drill a diagonal pilot hole through each bottom rung into the center of the slanted braces. Nail as before.

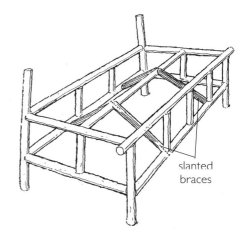

slanted braces

7. Attaching the Back and Seat Supports

Center the back support across the top of the back legs. Drill holes down through the support and into the legs. Fasten with 16d nails. Drill in-line pilot holes 1½ inches from each end and one in the center of the seat support. Position this piece in front and level with the top back rung. Nail it to the rung with 16d nails. (The seat and back rails will be nailed to this limb later.)

If you are making a porch swing, see the box on page 78 for how to fasten the chain support limbs now.

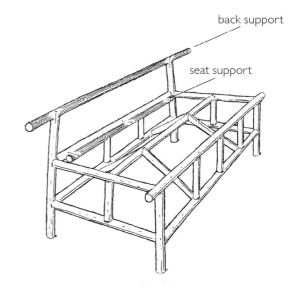

back support

seat support

Adapting the Loveseat into a Porch Swing

If you are making a porch swing, add the front and rear chair supports after finishing step 7.

A. Place the front chain support piece beneath the top side rungs, centered against the front legs. Holding the piece firmly in place, drill ⅛" pilot holes through the center of the front legs and *slightly* into the front chain support. Remove the support and deepen the pilot holes. Then return the support to its original position, line up the drilled holes, and nail with 16d nails.

   Measure in 2" on the *top* of each end of the front chain support and drill a ⅜" hole through the piece as squarely as possible. Place a plain washer on two eye bolts and insert the bolts down through the ⅜" holes. Place the (large) fender washers, then the nuts, on the bottom of the eye bolts. Tighten the nuts until the washers are snug against the wood. *Do not overtighten.*

B. Measure down from the top of each back leg 2½" and drill a ⅜" hole from the front to the back. Center the rear chain support against the back of the back legs over the holes you drilled. Drill back through the holes and slightly into the rear chain support to mark the location of the holes. Remove the support and drill ⅜" holes through the support on the drill marks.

Attach the rear chain support to the back legs using the 5½" carriage bolts, running them in from the front of the swing. Put the plain washers and lock nuts on the bolts and tighten snugly against the wood. *Do not overtighten.*

   Measure in 2" on the *top* of each end of the rear chain support and drill a ⅜" hole through the piece as squarely as possible. Place a plain washer on two eye bolts, and insert the bolts down through the ⅜" holes. Place the (large) fender washers, then the nuts, on the bottom of the eye bolts. Tighten the nuts until the washers are snug against the wood. Do not overtighten.

❧ If you intend to use this willow piece only as a porch swing, you may trim the legs close to the bottom front and back rungs. It would be best to do this when you have completed all twelve project steps.

❧ Attach and adjust the chains to finish your swing.

rear chain support

front chain support

8. Attaching the First Two Arm Benders

Drill a $\frac{1}{16}$" pilot hole and, with a 6d nail, fasten the butt end of an arm bender to the *inside* of the front bottom rung. The bender should lean against the inside of the front leg. Wrap the arm piece up and tuck it under the back support, against the back leg. Drill another $\frac{1}{16}$" pilot hole, nail the bender to the back support, and trim off the extra length.

Now attach an arm bender on the other side of the loveseat using the same method.

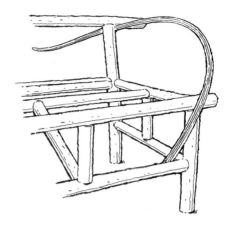

Splicing Benders

You may need to splice some of the arm and back benders to make them long enough. You can find information on splicing in chapter 2, page 26.

9. Completing the Arms

Put three additional benders on each side. Alternate the sides to keep the frame from warping. Nail the benders to each other every 6 to 8 inches with 1" or $1\frac{5}{8}$" paneling nails as required to maintain the contour. Remember to stagger the nails for each layer.

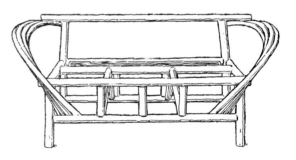

10. Preparing the template

Draw a straight line across the plywood template 4" from the bottom. Measure the distance from outside edge to outside side of the arm benders, and mark this distance on the line drawn on the template. Trim off the excess plywood.

Now measure the width of the arm benders on each side, and mark these measurements on each end of the template line. Notch the template to fit between the arm benders.

Mark the center of the line between the notches. Measure up 19", and mark this point directly above the last. Draw a sweeping arch from the topmost point to the outside edge of the arm benders. You may want to tape butcher's paper to the plywood and draw several arches from the 19" center line to one side. When you get the look you want, cut the arch out of the butcher's paper and trace it onto the plywood template. Then flip the paper arch over and trace the other half of the arch on the other side.

Cut out the plywood template with a saw. Clamp or tack the template to the back legs.

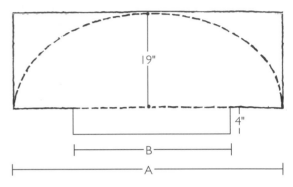

A. Distance from outer edge of left arm benders to outer edge of right arm benders.
B. Distance from inner edge of left arm benders to inner edge of right arm benders.

I I. Attaching the Back Benders

Clamp the plywood template to the back frame of the loveseat. The template will support the benders and give a nice, even shape to the back.

Drill a ¹⁄₁₆" pilot hole and, using a 6d nail, fasten the butt end of the first bender to the inside of the top side rung. Wrap the bender outside the arm, against the back support, and around the template. Drill a ¹⁄₁₆" pilot hole, and nail the bender to the inside of the top back rung on the other side. Trim off the extra length. Do not nail the first bender to the template.

Start the next bender on the opposite side and wrap it the other way. Alternating sides will give a more even shape to the back. Nail the second bender to the first using 1" or 1⁵⁄₈" paneling nails

back benders

every 6 to 8 inches, as required to maintain the contour. Remember to stagger the nails. When all four back benders are in place (and lined up along the side rungs), remove the template.

I2. Assembling the Seat and Back Rails

Measure the seat length from the outer edge of the top back rung to the front edge of the front top rung. Cut the first seat rail, and position it in the middle of the seat. Drill $1/16$" pilot holes, and nail the seat rail to the seat support, seat brace, and front rung with $1\,5/8$" paneling nails.

Now measure the center height of the back, from the base of the seat support to the top of the second back bender (measure from the *front* of the seat support to the *back* of the back bender). Cut a back rail to fit and position it next to the seat rail you just installed. Nail it with 1" or $1\,5/8$" paneling nails to the front of the back support and to the back of the first or second back bender.

Install the rest of the back and seat rails, working from the middle out to each side. Remember to put a seat rail on, then a back rail. *Because the back is wider at the top, the back rails will fan out.* Trim off the extra length.

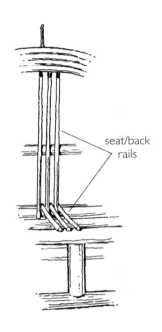

seat/back rails

I3. Attaching the Back Trim (optional)

Drill $1/16$" pilot holes about 4" apart in the back trim piece. Using 1" or $1\,5/8$" paneling nails, nail the back trim to the back benders on the back of the loveseat. The trim piece creates a more finished look.

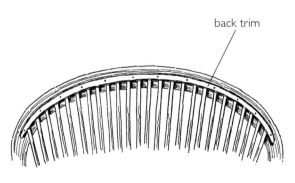

back trim

Lounger

Without a doubt, the lounger is the most creative and challenging project in this book. It will take awhile to complete, so pace yourself. Have a cool glass of iced tea ready so you can celebrate when you finish, then sit back, relax, and enjoy.

Remember, as with all willow projects, you are working with natural contours. Take advantage of the uniqueness of each piece of willow. Before you cut the material for the frame, lay all the pieces on the floor and separate them by diameter, texture, color, and special features, such as attractive knots. If you need a straight piece, turn the limb around and look at its full profile. Place some bowed pieces on the bottom to fit your bottom! Soon you will develop an eye for willow that you will use when harvesting for all projects.

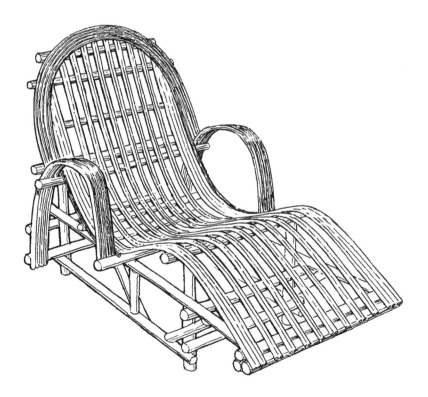

Materials				
Part	Quantity	Diameter	Length	Type of Wood
Left and Right Side Frame				
back legs	2	$1\frac{1}{2}$"	35"	seasoned
front legs	2	$1\frac{1}{2}$"	$15\frac{3}{4}$"	seasoned
bottom rails	2	$1\frac{1}{2}$"	42"	seasoned
top rails	2	$1\frac{1}{2}$"	52"	seasoned
front braces	2	$1\frac{1}{2}$"	cut to fit (approx. 14")	seasoned
back braces	2	$1\frac{1}{2}$"	cut to fit (approx. 40")	seasoned
back support braces	2	$1\frac{1}{2}$"	$7\frac{1}{2}$"	seasoned
seat supports	2	$1\frac{1}{2}$"	cut to fit (approx. 8")	seasoned
Side Frames Connectors				
top front cross rail	1	$1\frac{1}{2}$"	24"	seasoned
top rear cross rail	1	$1\frac{1}{2}$"	31"	seasoned
front top rail support	1	$1\frac{1}{2}$"	20"	seasoned
rear top rail support	1	$1\frac{1}{2}$"	31"	seasoned
front bottom cross rail	1	$1\frac{1}{2}$"	20"	seasoned
rear bottom cross rail	1	$1\frac{1}{2}$"	31"	seasoned
Frame Braces				
side frame brace	1	1"	approx. 48"	seasoned
back leg brace	1	1"	27"	seasoned
front leg brace	1	1"	20"	seasoned
Seat Rails				
seat rail #1	1	$1\frac{1}{2}$"	24"	seasoned
seat rail #1A	1	$1\frac{1}{2}$"	24"	seasoned
seat rail #1B	1	$1\frac{1}{2}$"	24"	seasoned
seat rail #2	1	$1\frac{1}{2}$"	31"	seasoned
seat rail #3	1	1"	24"	seasoned
seat rail #4	1	$1\frac{1}{2}$"	24"	seasoned
seat rail #5	1	$1\frac{1}{2}$"	31"	seasoned
seat rail #6	1	$1\frac{1}{2}$"	24"	seasoned
seat rail #7	1	$1\frac{1}{2}$"	31"	seasoned
Benders				
arm benders	8	$\frac{3}{4}$"	53"	flexible
back bender support rail	1	2"	31"	seasoned
back benders	4	$\frac{3}{4}$"	65"	flexible
seat benders	18	$\frac{1}{2}$"	76"	flexible
seat bender trim	1	$\frac{3}{4}$"	95"	flexible

template: 1 piece of $\frac{3}{4}$" plywood, 24" × 24"
clamps: 2 clamps, 4" size

I. Beginning the Side Frames

Mark the *smaller* end of each back and front leg; this will be the *top* of the leg. Measuring up from the bottom, place in-line marks on the *side* of each at 2¾" and 10¾", and additionally on each back leg at 22¾" and 26". Now drill ⅛" pilot holes into each leg at these locations. Also drill a ⅛" pilot hole down into the center of each leg's top end.

Measure in 2¾" from both ends of the two bottom rails and drill in-line pilot holes in each.

Select one front leg, one back leg, and one bottom rail for the left side frame. Lay the legs on a flat surface with the bottoms toward you and the back leg on your *right* side. Lay the bottom rail on top of the legs, align the rail's pilot holes with the lower pair of leg holes, and nail the pieces together with 16d nails.

Lay the other front leg, back leg, and bottom rail on a flat surface with the bottoms toward you and the back leg on your *left* side. You are now ready to begin assembling the right side frame. Lay the second bottom rail on top of the legs, align the pilot holes, and nail with 16d nails.

Measuring from what will be the *back ends* of the top rails, mark and drill in-line pilot holes in each at 2¾" and 39¼". Lay one rail on top of the left side frame, align the rail and leg pilot holes as illustrated, and nail with 16d nails. Now, square the rails and legs with each other. Repeat for the right side frame.

Note on Pilot Holes

Drill all pilot holes for this project with a ⅛" bit, unless otherwise specified. (The benders in steps 12 through 17 take ¹⁄₁₆" pilot holes.)

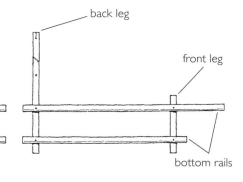

back leg

front leg

bottom rails

2. Cutting the Back and Front Braces

Begin with the left side frame. Measure up from the bottom of the back leg 26¼" and mark the front side. Then measure from the front end of the bottom rail 15¾" and mark the top edge. Lay a back brace diagonally across the top and bottom rails and the back leg, with the *top edge* of the back brace on the marks. Draw a line on the back brace, even with the front edge of the back leg, and then cut this diagonal. Cut the bottom off square 1" past the lower edge of the bottom rail.

Measure in from the front end of the top rail 6½" and mark the *bottom* of the top rail. Then measure in from the front end of the bottom rail 4" and mark the *top* edge. Lay a front brace diagonally across the top and bottom rails, with the *front edge* of the brace on the marks. Draw a line for diagonal cuts even with the top edge of the bottom rail and the bottom edge of the top rail. Cut the brace to fit.

Repeat this entire step for the right side frame (a mirror maze of the left side frame).

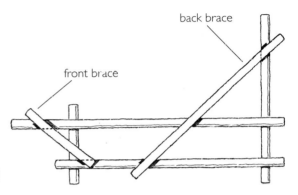

back brace

front brace

3. Installing the Back and Front Braces

Begin with the left side frame. Slip the back brace under the top and bottom rails and butt the angle cut against the front edge of the back leg, with the top edge of the brace on the mark. Also, place the front surface of the brace at the mark you made on the bottom rail. Square the rails and legs with each other and check the position of the back brace to be sure it is on the marks. Hold the back brace centered on the back leg and drill a pilot hole through the center of the leg into the center of the back brace. Angle the hole to match the angle of the brace. Nail the piece in place with a 16d nail.

Check to be sure the rails and legs are still square with each other. Then drill a pilot hole through the center of the bottom rail into the center of the back brace and nail with a 16d nail. Repeat for the top rail.

Lay the front brace in position. Drill angled pilot holes through the center of the top and bottom rails into the center of the front brace. Nail with 16d nails.

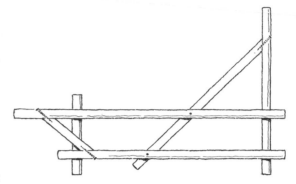

4. Completing the Side Frames

Begin with the left side frame. Measure in 5" from one end of what will be the top of the back support brace, and drill a pilot hole. Lay the back support brace across the back brace and back leg, aligning the pilot hole with the next-to-highest hole (the one at 22¾") you drilled in the back leg in step 1. Fasten with a 16d nail.

Now, adjust the back support brace until it is square with (perpendicular to) the back brace. To avoid splitting the wood, drill a pilot hole through the center of the back support brace into the back brace at an angle *away from* the end of the back brace. Nail with a 16d nail.

Prop the assembly upright. Measure from the front end of the top rail 24" back. At this mark, measure the distance between the top and bottom

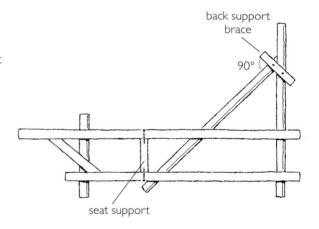

back support brace

90°

seat support

rails, and cut a seat support to fit here. Center the seat support piece on the mark. Drill a pilot hole through the top rail into the center of the seat support, and nail this piece in place with a 16d nail.

Now turn the assembly upside down. Adjust the seat support piece until it is square with the rails. Drill a pilot hole through the bottom rail into the center of the seat support, and nail this end in place with a 16d nail.

Repeat this entire step for the right side frame.

5. Attaching the Top Cross Rails

Prop the side frames upright on a flat surface with the rails to the outside. Measure in from each end of the top front cross rail 4" and drill in-line pilot holes.

Drive a 16d nail through one of these holes until it sticks out slightly on the other side. Center the protruding nail point in the pilot hole you previously drilled (in step 1) into the top end of a front leg. Drive the nail in. Repeat this process for the other front leg. The side frame assembly should stand on its own now.

Measure in 7½" from each end of the top rear cross rail and drill in-line pilot holes. Drive a 16d nail through one of these holes until it slightly sticks out on the other side. Center the protruding nail point over a back leg. Drive this nail in. Repeat this process for the other back leg.

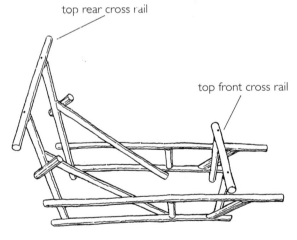

top rear cross rail

top front cross rail

6. Attaching the Top Rail Supports

Measure in 2" from each end of the front top rail support piece and drill in-line pilot holes all the way through. Position the rail support underneath the top rails and against the front side of the front legs. (You can stand the assembly on its back if you wish.) Center the right hole on the leg and hold the support tightly against the top rail. Drill back through the holes and slightly into the legs. Remove the rail support piece and drill pilot holes through the front legs. Nail the support to the front legs with 16d nails.

Check the front legs to be sure they are square. Adjust if necessary.

Measure in 7½" from each end of the rear top rail support piece and drill in-line pilot holes. Position this piece underneath the top rails and against the front side of the back legs. Center the right hole on the leg and hold the support tightly against the top rail. As you did for the front support, drill back through the holes and slightly into the legs. Remove the support piece and drill pilot holes through the back legs. Nail the support to the back legs with 16d nails.

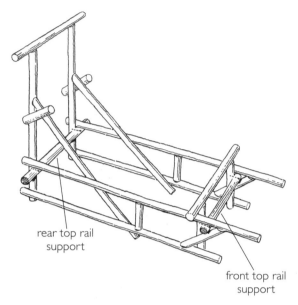

rear top rail support

front top rail support

7. Attaching the Bottom Cross Rails

Measure in 2" from each end of the front bottom cross rail piece and drill in-line pilot holes. Position this piece *on top of* the bottom rails and against the front side of the front legs. Center the right hole on the leg and hold the cross rail tightly against the bottom rail.

Drill back through the holes and slightly into the legs. Remove the cross rail piece and drill pilot holes through the front legs. Nail the cross rail to the front legs with 16d nails.

Measure in 7½" from each end of the rear bottom cross rail piece and drill in-line pilot holes. Position this piece *on top of* the bottom rails and against the front side of the back legs. Center the right hole on the leg and hold the cross rail tightly against the bottom rail. As before, drill back through the holes and slightly into the legs. Remove the cross rail piece and drill pilot holes through the back legs. Nail the cross rail to the back legs with 16d nails.

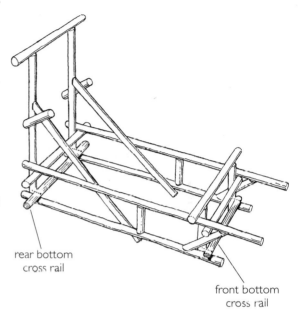

rear bottom
cross rail

front bottom
cross rail

8. Installing a Temporary Side Brace

In steps 8–10 you will install three temporary braces. Turn the frame upside down. Measure from the center of a back leg diagonally across to the center of the opposite front leg. Then repeat for the other two legs. *These diagonal measurements must be the same for the frame to be square.* Adjust the frame until they match. Remember that adjusting one side will affect the other, so be sure you recheck both measurements after each adjustment.

Tack the side frame brace to a bottom rail where it meets the corresponding back leg. Use an 8d nail driven just deep enough to hold the frame square. Position the brace diagonally across the frame, to where the other bottom rail meets the corresponding front leg. Tack the brace on this side, but first check the frame once again to be sure it is square.

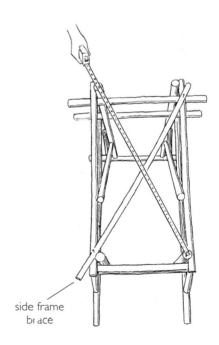

side frame
brace

9. Installing a Temporary Back Leg Brace

With the frame still upside down, turn it so you face the back. Measure from the center of the end of the top rail diagonally across to the center of the end of the opposite bottom rail. Repeat for the other pair of rails. *These diagonal measurements must be the same for the frame to be square.* Adjust the frame until they match. Again, remember that adjusting one side will affect the other, so be sure you recheck both measurements after each adjustment.

Position the temporary back leg brace on top of a bottom rail and against the back leg, and lay it diagonally across to the bottom of the back support brace on the opposite leg. Tack the temporary brace in place (to the leg only) on one end with an 8d nail. Check to be sure the assembly is still square, and then tack the other end (to the leg only).

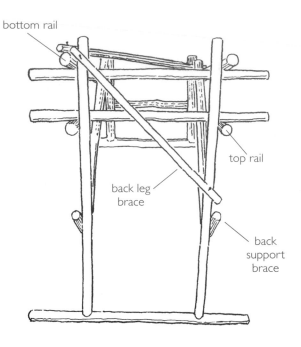

bottom rail

top rail

back leg brace

back support brace

10. Installing a Temporary Front Leg Brace

Lay the assembly on its back. Measure from the inside corner of the top front cross rail where it meets the top of one of the front legs, diagonally across to the inside corner of the bottom end of the opposite front leg. Repeat for the other side. *These diagonal measurements must be the same for the frame to be square.* Adjust the frame until they match. Using an 8d nail, tack one end of the brace to the top rail support, 1" from the end. In the same manner, tack the brace's other end to the front bottom cross rail. Check to be sure the assembly is still square, and then nail the other end.

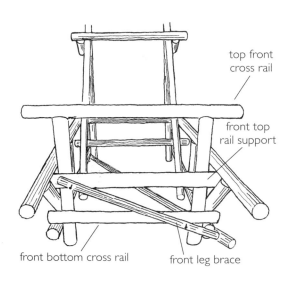

top front cross rail

front top rail support

front bottom cross rail

front leg brace

Now turn the frame upright on a flat surface and look at it from all sides. The legs should be flat on the floor. If the frame tips, adjust it up or down until it sets square and solid on the flat surface. Make any other final adjustments now.

11. Installing the Seat Rails

In this step you will install a total of nine seat rails across the width of the frame (see illustration on page 92).

Seat Rail 1

Center seat rail 1 across the frame *on the front ends* of the top rails. Holding the limb firmly in place, mark where it intersects the center ends of the top rails. Remove the seat rail and drill in-line pilot holes through the diameter of the limb. Reposition the seat rail and drill back through one of the pilot holes slightly into the end of the top rail. Remove the seat rail and finish drilling the pilot hole into top rail.

Tack (do not nail it in all the way yet) seat rail 1 in place with a 16d nail. Then drill back through the other pilot hole to mark the drill location on the second top rail. Swing the seat rail out of the way and finish drilling the pilot hole into the end of the second top rail. Now nail seat rail 1 firmly in place.

Seat Rail 1A

Place in-line marks 3" from each end of seat rail 1A and halfway between. Drill pilot holes at all three locations.

Note on Hardware

Nail all nine seat rails in place with 16d nails.

Place seat rail 1A *below* seat rail 1 with the ends flush and the drilled holes oriented so you can drill into seat rail 1. Clamp seat rail 1A firmly in place (two 4" clamps should be adequate). Drill back through first pilot hole and slightly into seat rail 1.

Remove the clamps and seat rail 1A, and complete the pilot hole in seat rail 1. Tack seat rail 1A back in place, and then drill back through the other two pilot holes to mark their locations on seat rail 1. Swing seat rail 1A aside and finish drilling the pilot holes in seat rail 1. Nail seat rail 1A in place.

Seat Rail 1B

Place in-line marks 2" from each end of seat rail 1B and halfway between. Drill in-line pilot holes *slightly off these marks* toward either end; drilling slightly off to the side will help you avoid hitting the nails in seat rail 1A when you nail them together.

Clamp seat rail 1B *in front of* seat rail 1A with the ends flush, and the pilot holes oriented so you can drill into seat rail 1A. Drill back through the first pilot hole and slightly into seat rail 1A.

Remove the clamps and seat rail 1B, and complete the pilot hole in seat rail 1A. Tack seat rail 1B back in place, and then drill back through the other two pilot holes to mark their locations on seat rail 1A. Swing seat rail 1B aside and finish drilling the pilot holes in seat rail 1A. Nail seat rail 1B in place.

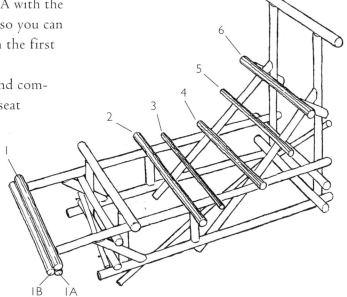

Seat Rail 2

Mark the outside of the top rails 23¾" back from the front end of each. You may need to move these marks slightly off to one side to avoid hitting the fasteners in the seat supports when you nail the seat rail in place.

Center seat rail 2 across the frame on the marks. Drill pilot holes through the center of the seat rail into the top rails at a slight angle, from the inside of the top rail to the outside. These holes are drilled at an angle to avoid splitting the top rails. Nail seat rail 2 in place.

Seat Rail 3

Mark the outside of the top rails 28" back from the front end of each. Measure in 2" from each end of seat rail 3 and drill in-line pilot holes.

Center seat rail 3 across the frame on the marks. Holding the seat rail firmly in place, drill back through one of the pilot holes slightly into the top rail.

Remove seat rail 3 and finish drilling the pilot hole in the top rail. Now, *tack* seat rail 3 in place with a nail. Drill back through the other pilot hole slightly into the other top rail. Swing seat rail 3 aside and finish drilling the pilot hole in the top rail. Nail seat rail 3 in place.

Seat Rails 4 and 5

Measure down from the top of the back braces (where the top edge of each back brace meets a back leg) 18½". Mark the outside of the back braces.

Make similar marks 10½" down. Center seat rail 4 across the frame on the lower pair of marks. Holding seat rail 4 firmly in place, mark the center of the seat rail where it intersects the center of the back braces. Remove seat rail 4 and drill in-line pilot holes on these marks.

Now, put seat rail 4 back in position and drill back through one of the pilot holes slightly into the back brace. Remove seat rail 4 and finish drilling the pilot hole in the back brace. *Tack* seat rail 4 in place with a nail. Then drill back through the other seat rail pilot hole and slightly into the other back brace. Swing seat rail 4 aside and finish drilling the pilot hole. Nail seat rail 4 in place.

Center seat rail 5 across the frame on the upper pair of marks (10½" down from the top of the back braces) you made. Proceed as you did for seat rail 4.

Seat Rail 6

Center seat rail 6 across the frame *on the ends* of the back support braces. Holding it firmly in place, mark the center of the rail where it intersects the center ends of the braces. Remove the seat rail and drill in-line pilot holes on these marks.

Now, put seat rail 6 back in position and proceed exactly as you did when attaching seat rails 4 and 5 to the back brace.

Seat Rail 7

Mark the outside of the back legs 2¾" down from the top. Center seat rail 7 across the frame on the marks. Holding it firmly in place, mark the center of the rail where it intersects the back legs.

Remove seat rail 7 and drill in-line pilot holes on these marks.

Now, put seat rail 7 back in position and proceed exactly as you did when attaching seat rails 4, 5, and 6 to their various locations.

12. Attaching the First Pair of Arm Benders

Measure in 3" from each end of seat rail 2, seat rail 5, the rear bottom cross rail, and the rear top rail support, and mark these locations on the top of these pieces. Place the butt end of an arm bender against the front of the rear bottom cross rail, with the end 1" past the bottom of this rail. Position the inside edge of the bender on the 3" mark. Drill a $\frac{1}{16}$" pilot hole through the bender and the rear bottom cross rail and nail with a $1\frac{5}{8}$" paneling nail. Now, align the inside edge of the bender with the 3" mark on the rear top rail support. As before, drill a $\frac{1}{16}$" pilot hole through the bender and the rear top rail support and nail.

Bend the arm bender over the top of seat rail 5 and tuck it behind seat rail 2, with the inside edge of the bender on the 3" marks. Clamp the bender at both seat rails and then step back to check its shape. It is important to shape this first arm bender well because the rest of the arm benders will be formed to it. The top side should be relatively flat but slightly higher at the front; the peak should be about $12\frac{1}{2}$" above the top of the top side rail. Let the front bend radius go past seat rail 2. Make adjustments to get the shape you want. Then, holding the bender in position, remove the clamp at seat

Splicing Benders

You may need to splice some of the arm, back, or seat benders to make them long enough. See chapter 2, page 26, for information on splicing.

rail 5. Drill a $\frac{1}{16}$" pilot hole and nail the bender to seat rail 5 with a $1\frac{5}{8}$" paneling nail.

Again holding the bender in position, remove the clamp at seat rail 2, drill a $\frac{1}{16}$" pilot hole, and nail the bender in place with a $1\frac{5}{8}$" paneling nail.

Next, install a second arm bender on the other side of the lounger using the same method. Be sure you match the shape of the first bender as closely as possible.

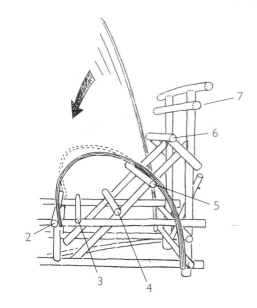

13. Installing the Seat of the Arm Bender and the Back Bender Support Rail

Put four arm benders on each side. Alternate sides to avoid warping the frames. Keep the benders even with each other. Nail the arm benders to each other, and to the rails, every 6" to 8" with 1" or $1\frac{5}{8}$" paneling nails, as required to maintain the contour. Remember to stagger the nails for each layer. Trim off the excess length of the arm benders $\frac{1}{2}$" past the bottom of seat rail 2.

Place the back bender support rail on top of the arm benders and the back braces. Make the ends flush with seat rail 5. Drill $\frac{1}{8}$" pilot holes through the center of the back bender support rail and slightly into the back braces. Remove the support rail and finish drilling the pilot holes through the back braces. Nail the back bender support rail to the back braces with 16d nails.

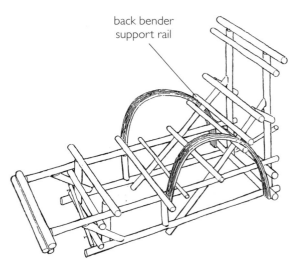

back bender support rail

14. Preparing a Template for the Back Benders

Draw a line across the plywood template 6" from the bottom. Mark the center of this line. Use a scrap piece of willow ½" to ¾" in diameter and about 15" long. Measure from one end 12" and drive a nail through the center of the scrap. Place the point of the nail on the center mark of the template line and drive it in just enough to allow the willow piece to pivot. Hold a pencil against the long end of the willow piece and mark an arch on the template. Remove the scrap piece and discard it. Cut out the template with a saw.

Clamp or tack the template to the back bender support rail, centered between the arms and with the bottom of the template even with the top of the arm benders.

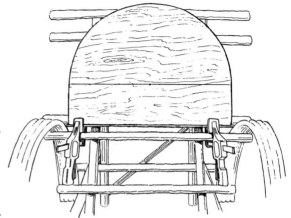

15. Attaching the Back Benders

Position the butt end of the first back bender against the top of the left or right inside arm bender and the edge of the template. Drill a ⅟₁₆" pilot hole and nail it to the back bender support rail with a 1⅝" paneling nail. Wrap the bender around the template and tuck it inside the other arm. Now, trim the bender about 1" longer than you think you need to butt the end flush with the arm bender. Continue trimming small amounts off the back bender until it is tight against the template and arm. Drill several ⅟₁₆" pilot holes and nail the back bender where it intersects seat rails 6 and 7, and to the top rear cross rail, using 1⅝" paneling nails.

Do not nail the back bender to the template, which you will remove when all the back benders are in place.

Start the next back bender on the opposite side and wrap it the other way. Alternating sides will give a more even shape to the back. Nail the second back bender to the first one, and to the rails, with 1" or 1⅝" paneling nails every 6" to 8", as required to maintain the contour. Remember to stagger the nails. After placing all four back benders, remove the template.

16. Attaching the Seat Benders

Mark the center of all nine seat rails and the top front cross rail. Measure from this center mark 9¾" on each side, and mark the top side of the rails. Place the butt end of the first seat bender against the front edge of seat rail 1B, with the inside edge on either the left or right mark. Let the bender overhang the front of the seat rail about 2".

Drill ¹⁄₁₆" pilot holes through the bender into seat rail 1B and seat rail 1, and then nail it with 1⅝" paneling nails. Bend it toward the back over the top front cross rail. Align the inside edge of the seat bender with the rail mark, drill a ¹⁄₁₆" pilot hole, and nail with a 1⅝" paneling nail.

Repeat the procedure with seat rail 2. Push the seat bender up to seat rail 4, making sure the bender lies against seat rail 3. Drill and nail as before, first to seat rail 4 and then to seat rail 3. Now, trim the bender even with the *bottom* edge of the back bender and nail it to the remaining intersecting seat rails.

Nail a second seat bender on the other side of the lounger using the same method. It is important to alternate sides to keep from warping the frame.

Lay another seat bender against the outside of the first one, alternating the butt ends to get a more uniform look. Continue placing seat benders until you have three or four on each side. The number you use will depend on the diameter of the seat benders. Use three seat benders to begin with and add another one later to make the spacing more uniform, if needed.

Now, measure and mark ¾" on each side of the center marks you made on the rails. Position two seat benders on each side, with the *inside edge* of these pairs on the ¾" mark. Using the same procedure as before, drill pilot holes and nail the paired bender in place all the way up to the top rear cross rail. Then evenly space and fasten the remaining benders in pairs between the benders on the edge and those in the center. When all the seat benders are in place, trim off the bottom edges evenly.

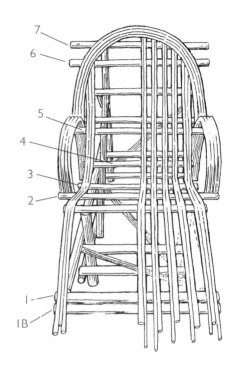

17. Trimming and Finishing

Drill a ¹⁄₁₆" pilot hole and nail the butt end of the seat bender trim piece to seat rail 2 with 1⅝" paneling nails. Bend it up and around the inside of the innermost back bender to hide the cut ends of the seat benders. Drill ¹⁄₁₆" pilot holes and nail the trim to intersecting rails and seat benders with 1" or 1⅝" paneling nails.

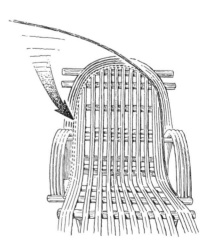

Grandma's Fan
Double Bed Headboard

This design was inspired by a quilt pattern called grandma's fan. We used an advanced mortise technique to hide the ends of the willow benders in the posts and rails. Brian carefully chose a post with a jutting limb at the top for his side of the bed. This is where he would hang his hat!

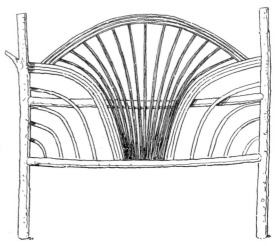

Materials				
Part	Quantity	Diameter	Length	Type of Wood
posts	2	3"	52"	seasoned
rails	2	1½"	55"	seasoned
side rim benders	2	¾"	34½"	flexible
	2	¾"	35¾"	flexible
	2	¾"	37"	flexible
side fill benders	2	½"	26¾"	flexible
	2	½"	20½"	flexible
	2	½"	13¾"	flexible
	2	½"	7⅜"	flexible
center rim benders	3	¾"	60"	flexible
center fill benders	13	½"	approx. 36"	flexible

template: 1 piece of ¾" plywood 18" × 48"

bolts: 4 lag bolts, ¼ × 5" long

washers: 4 plain

1. Preparing the Posts and Rails

Lay the posts on a flat surface with the most attractive side out. Measure up from the bottom post 18" and 32", and mark these locations in the center *inside* of each post. Now roll the posts over so the marks are on top.

Measure the diameter of the ends of the rails and *for each rail* choose a spade or paddle bit that is nearest to the *smaller of these diameters.* Wrap a piece of tape (electrician's tape works well) around the bit(s), ½" up from the tip. Now, drill holes as squarely as possible in the posts at the 18" and 32" marks, *stopping when the tape touches the wood.* Changing to a ¼" bit, drill a pilot hole on through the posts in the center of these countersunk holes.

Measure the diameter of the washers you will be using when you bolt the posts and rails together (in step 2). Choose a spade or paddle bit equal to or slightly larger than this diameter. Again, wrap tape around the bit, ½" up from the tip. Centering on the ¼" pilot hole, drill countersunk holes in the *outside* of the posts to the depth of the tape.

Note on Post Holes

For rails with thicker diameters you may choose to use a hole saw instead of a drill when preparing the post holes. If so, remove the wood from the hole with a chisel.

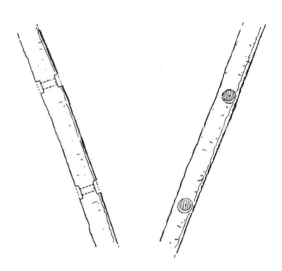

2. Assembling the Posts and Rails

If necessary, whittle the ends of the rails to fit the inside post holes, and insert the rails. Tap the posts onto the rails until they sit fully in the countersunk holes.

Now, from the outside of the posts drill ³⁄₁₆"
holes back through the ¼" pilot holes and slightly
into the center ends of the rails. Remove the rails
from the posts and drill ³⁄₁₆" pilot holes in the ends
of the rails where you marked them with the drill.
Make these holes at least 3" deep. Reinsert the rails
in the post holes and bolt the posts to the rails
using ¼" × 5" lag bolts with washers.

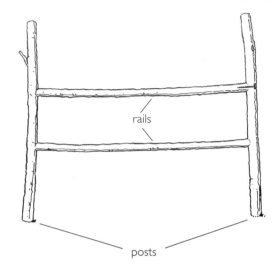

rails

posts

3. Preparing the Frame for Benders

Measuring from the inside of each post, mark the
top side of the bottom rail at 20½". Select a ¾"
spade or paddle bit. As before, wrap tape ½" up
from the tip, and then drill a hole at each mark to
the depth of the tape. Draw a line from the center
of one hole to the center of the other hole. Now,
drill a series of holes on this line slightly overlapping each other to make a channel in the rail. Here
again, drill these holes to the depth of the tape. You
will then need to chisel out some areas to square
the channel along the sides.

Mark the inside of each post 20½" and 22" up
from the top of the bottom rail. Using the ¾"
spade or paddle bit, drill holes at these locations,
then connect them as before to make channels in
the posts.

Measuring from the inside of each post, mark the
top of the bottom rail at 4", 8", 12", and 16".
Select a ½" spade or paddle bit and wrap tape ½"

up from the tip. Drill holes in the top of the bottom rail at all eight marks. *Do not connect these holes.*

Measuring up from the top of the bottom rail, mark the inside of each post at these locations: 4", 8", 12", and 16". Use the ½" spade or paddle bit to drill holes at these locations. *Do not connect these holes.*

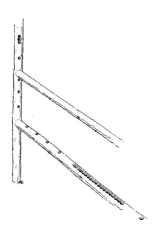

4. Attaching the Side Benders

Place the butt end of the 34½" side rim bender in the channel in the bottom rail and slide it as far as you can toward one of the posts. Drill a ¹⁄₁₆" pilot hole at an angle through the bender into the bottom rail. Nail it in place with a 1⅝" paneling nail.

Bend the side rim bender and insert the other end into the channel on the appropriate post. Slide it down to the bottom of the channel. Drill a ¹⁄₁₆" pilot hole at an angle through the bender into the post. Nail it in place with a 1⅝" paneling nail. *Do not nail the bender to the top rail yet.*

Repeat this process, placing the other 34½" side rim bender on the other side.

Now, check the posts and rails to be sure they are square. Also check the curve of the benders for uniformity. Drill a ¹⁄₁₆" pilot hole through the side rim benders into the center diameter of the top rail. Nail the benders in place with 1⅝" paneling nails.

Place the 35¾" rim benders beside the first bender pair, wrapping and nailing at 6" to 8" intervals with 1⅝" paneling nails. (Be sure to drill pilot holes first, and nail into rail and posts, as well.)

Nailing the Headboard Benders

You may need to use a nail set to drive angled nails completely into the rail and posts.

Remember to stagger the nails and alternate the butt ends. You may need to trim the length of the benders to get them to lay flat. Trim *small* amounts off and check the fit as you go. Repeat for the 37" rim benders.

Place the side fill benders in the holes you drilled in the bottom rail and corresponding post on each side. You may need to whittle some off the ends of the benders to get a good fit in the hole. *Do not nail them in place yet.*

Stand away from the headboard and check the shape of the benders. Adjust them until they please your eye and both sides are symmetrical.

Now, drill $\frac{1}{16}$" pilot holes through the side fill benders and nail them on both ends with $1\frac{5}{8}$" paneling nails. Also, drill $\frac{1}{16}$" pilot holes and nail to the top rail benders that intersect it.

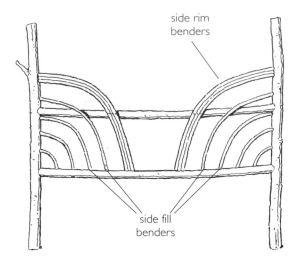

side rim benders

side fill benders

5. Preparing the Template

Lay the headboard on a flat surface. Center the plywood template on the top rail and clamp it to the side rim benders. Put corresponding reference marks on the center of the top rail and on the center of the template. These reference marks will be used to realign the template later. Also mark the center of the bottom rail.

Using a *straight* scrap piece of willow 34" long (about $\frac{3}{4}$" diameter), measure from one end 2" and drive a nail through the center on this mark. Place the end of the nail on the center mark of the bottom rail and drive it in just enough to allow the willow piece to pivot on the nail. Hold a pencil against the 32" end of the willow piece and mark an arch on the plywood template. Remove the scrap willow piece and discard it. Then, remove the template and extend the ends of the arched lines to the edge of the plywood on each side. Cut out the template.

Clamp the template back on the headboard, lining up the center reference marks. Turn the headboard over (back side up) and set it on blocks to protect it from scuffing and to raise the clamps off the floor.

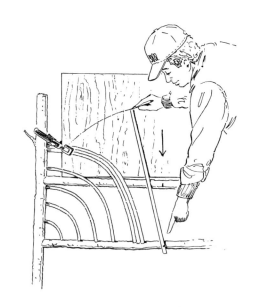

6. Positioning the Center Rim Benders

Place the butt end of the first center rim bender on top of the template and across the back of the side rim benders. Line up the end of the center rim bender and the bottom edge of the bottom side rim bender. Drill a $\frac{1}{16}$" pilot hole through the center rim bender into the top and middle side rim benders and nail the piece in place with $1\frac{5}{8}$" paneling nails.

Wrap this bender around the edge of the template. Holding the bender in place, trim this side off at the bottom edge of the bottom side rim bender. Drill $\frac{1}{16}$" pilot holes and nail this end to the top and middle side rim benders with $1\frac{5}{8}$" paneling nails. *Do not nail the bender to the template.*

Place the second center rim bender on top of this first bender, wrapping and nailing at 6" to 8" intervals with $1\frac{5}{8}$" paneling nails. (Nail into side rim benders, as well.) Remember to stagger the nails and alternate the butt ends. Repeat for the third center rim bender.

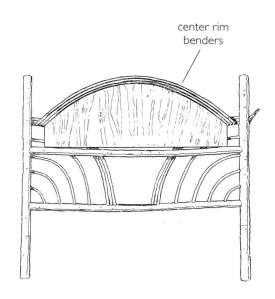

center rim benders

7. Positioning the Center Fill Benders

Turn the headboard back over (front side up) and find the center of the center arch. To do this, put a nail back into the hole in the bottom rail that you used to draw the arch on the template, attach a string, line it up with the center reference mark on the template, and stretch it to the top of the arch. Make a mark there. Now, remove the string, nail, and template.

Center the butt end of the first center fill bender into the channel in the bottom rail. Extend the bender across the front of the top rail and *behind* the arch. Drill a $\frac{1}{16}$" pilot hole at an angle through the bender into the bottom rail, and nail it in place with a $1\frac{5}{8}$" paneling nail. Align the bender over the center marks. Drill a $\frac{1}{16}$" pilot hole and nail it to the back of the middle center rim bender with a $1\frac{5}{8}$" paneling nail. Making sure the bender is straight, drill a $\frac{1}{16}$" pilot hole and also nail it to the top rail with a $1\frac{5}{8}$" paneling nail.

Now, put six center fill benders on each side of this center bender with the butt ends in the channel on the bottom rail. Evenly space these benders in the channel on each side.

Drill $\frac{1}{16}$" pilot holes at an angle through the butt end of each center fill bender into the bottom rail. Nail with $1\frac{5}{8}$" paneling nails. Evenly space these benders across the top arch in a fan shape. Drill $\frac{1}{16}$" pilot holes, alternating between the second and third rim benders to avoid splitting, and attach center fill benders to the top rail and to the center rim benders with $1\frac{5}{8}$" paneling nails. Trim the center fill benders slightly below the top edge of the top center rim bender.

Note on Center Fill Benders

If all the center fill benders do *not* fit in the bottom rail channel, try choosing some with smaller butt ends.

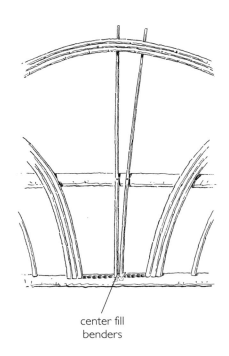

center fill benders

Tulip Mirror Frame

A tulip mirror frame hangs above an old steamer trunk in our entry hall. This piece is elegant, yet simple and very functional. The design looks best when you use very long benders — 98" to 108" — for the frame, but because these lengths are sometimes hard to find, the project text describes how to use shorter benders.

Materials				
Part	Quantity	Diameter	Length	Type of Wood
frame benders	4 or 5	¾"	50"	flexible
	8	¾"	cut to fit	flexible
frame trim	6	¾"	cut to fit	flexible
inside trim	2	½"	16½"	flexible
	2	½"	cut to fit	flexible
tulip trim	5	⅜" to ¼"	cut to fit	flexible

frame and template: 1 piece of ¾" plywood, 20½" × 34¼"

paint: 1 spray can of black or dark brown flat enamel

1. Preparing the Frame

Measure 2" in from each edge of the plywood piece and draw a rectangle all the way around. Also, near each corner measure in 2½" and mark short intersecting lines. Using a paddle bit (or a brace with a 1" auger bit), drill 1" holes centered on the inner intersecting lines.

Starting at one of the 1" holes, use an electric sabre saw or a hand keyhole saw to cut out the center of the frame along the 2" line, going from hole to hole. Save the center piece to use for a template in the next step.

Paint the plywood frame black or dark brown.

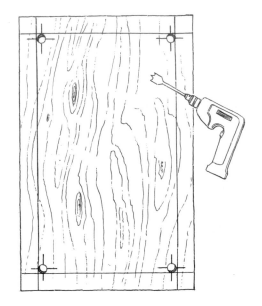

2. Cutting Out the Template

Using the center section of plywood you saved from step 1, draw a line across the width 2" in from the edge. Mark the center of this line.

Take a scrap piece of ¾" willow about 10" long and drive a nail through 8" from one end. Place the point of the nail on the center mark you made on the plywood and drive it in just enough to allow the willow piece to pivot. Hold a pencil against the 8" end of the scrap and scribe an arch on the template. Discard the scrap and cut out the template.

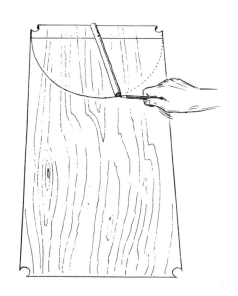

3. **Attaching the First Frame Bender**

Place the frame on a flat surface with the template centered on top. Align the straight side of the template with the inside edge of the frame. Lightly tack the template to the frame with 6d nails so you can remove it easily later.

Position the butt end of a 50" frame bender 4" down from the top of the left side of the frame, along the inside edge. Drill a ¹⁄₁₆" pilot hole 1" from this end of the bender, and then nail the bender to the frame with a 1⁵⁄₈" paneling nail. Drill another pilot hole and place a second nail 1½" from the first, staggered so you won't split the wood. *Do not nail the bender to the template.*

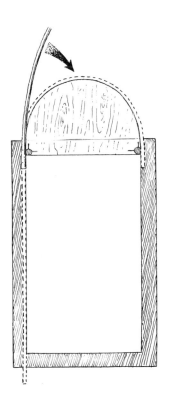

Wrap the bender tight around the top of the template. Drill two more pilot holes, 1" from the ends of the bender so you won't split the wood. With 1⁵⁄₈ paneling nails, nail the bender to the inside edge of the frame on the other side. Cut two matching (¾") bender pieces, one to complete the wrap down each side of the frame. Let these pieces run at least 1½" beyond the bottom of the frame.

4. **Installing the Rest of the Frame Benders**

Drill two pilot holes and nail the thickest end of a second 50" frame bender to the *right* side of the frame 4" from the top. Wrap this second bender tightly around the first, drill another pair of pilot holes, and nail it to the frame on the opposite side. Now, nail the second bender to the first one around the arch, drilling pilot holes and using 1⅝" paneling nails every 4".

Cut two matching pieces to fill the rest of the second wrap, again letting these pieces run at least 1½" off the bottom of the frame.

Start a third 50" frame bender on the *left* side, 8" from the top of the frame. Wrap, drill, and nail as you did for the second, and then fill the wrap with two more matching pieces.

Start the thickest end of the fourth 50" frame bender on the *right* side 10" from the top of the frame. Position it so that it touches the side of the frame and the side of the third wrap. Wrap, drill, nail, and fill as you did for the other benders.

The outermost wrap requires a slightly different procedure. You will need to place and nail these bender pieces carefully around the arch, being sure to cover the edge of the frame and ensuring that there are no gaps with previous benders. As before, these pieces run at least 1½" off the bottom of the frame. Start by placing the butt ends of two frame benders at the bottom of the frame, one on each side. Drill pilot holes and nail as before, but cut these benders off 4" from the top of the plywood frame. Finish the arch with a matching piece. Now, remove the template.

Note on Pilot Holes

Drill all pilot holes for this project with a ⅟₁₆" bit.

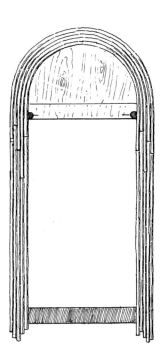

5. Installing the Frame Trim

Measure the horizontal space at the top of the frame, between the innermost frame benders. Cut three frame trim pieces to fit here. Slightly overlap the top and bottom edges of the frame to hide the plywood. Drill pilot holes, 1" from each end and one in the middle of each piece. Nail the trim pieces to the frame with 1⅝" paneling nails.

Now measure the horizontal space at the bottom of the frame and cut three additional frame trim pieces to fit. Put the top piece in first, slightly overlapping the inside edge of the frame to hide the plywood. Drill and nail the top and center pieces as you did the first three, but before you nail the bottom piece, set it in place and mark where its bottom edge meets the frame benders on each side. Remove the bottom frame trim piece and cut the frame benders even with the mark you just made. Put the bottom frame trim piece back in place, drill pilot holes, and nail it to the plywood frame.

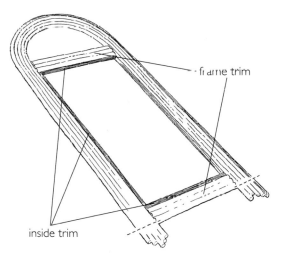

frame trim

inside trim

Lay the mirror frame on a flat surface. Drill pilot holes and, using 1⅝" paneling nails, nail the two 16½" inside trim pieces across the top and bottom of the inside frame opening. Be sure these pieces do not protrude past the back surface of the plywood frame or they will interfere with placement of the mirror.

Measure the two sides of the frame opening and cut the other flexible benders to fit. Nail them to the inside edge of the frame as you did the top and bottom inside trim pieces.

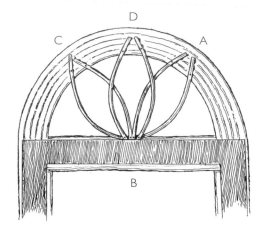

6. Installing the Tulip Trim

From the back side of the frame, find the center of the arch and mark it on the outside bender (point **D**). Also mark the midpoint of the plywood frame's top edge (**B**). Now, find the points halfway between the top of the arch and the base of the arch on each side, and label them **A** and **C**.

Tuck the end of a tulip trim bender underneath point **A**, drill pilot holes, and nail the trim piece with 1" paneling nails to the innermost frame benders. Bend it down to the top of the plywood frame at point **B** and around to point **C**, making a nice, even arc. Drill a pilot hole and nail it to the top of the plywood frame at **B**. Drill pilot holes and nail it to the innermost frame benders at **C**. Trim off the extra length.

Start another bender at point **B** on top of the trim piece you just installed. Arc this bender upward to **C**. Drill a pilot hole and nail it behind the innermost frame benders, and then trim off the excess length.

Begin another bender at **B** and arc this one to **A**. Drill a pilot hole, nail it as before, and trim off the excess length.

Start the center tulip trim piece at **B** outside the last two trim pieces you just put on and arc it to the right, to **D**. Drill, nail, and trim.

Begin the final tulip trim piece at **B** and arc it to the left, to **D**. Drill, nail, and trim.

Finally, take your tulip mirror frame to the local glass and mirror shop and have them professionally install a mirror in the frame.

Southwestern Mirror

Inspired by the Native American designs of the Southwest, this mirror frame is colorful and rustic. Use different colors of willow for the trim pieces or strip the bark on some pieces to make different designs in the pattern. You might also apply different paint or dyes on this design to match your decor.

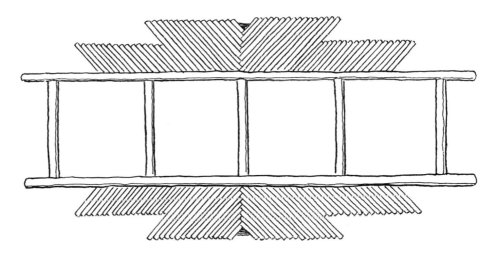

Materials				
Part	**Quantity**	**Diameter**	**Length**	**Type of Wood**
center trim	28	½"	12"	flexible
herringbone trim	13–16	½"	approx. 12"	flexible
edge trim	60	½"	7"	flexible
horizontal mirror trim	2 (straight)	1¼"	54½"	seasoned
vertical mirror trim	5	1¼"	cut to fit	seasoned

base: 1 piece of ¾" plywood, 26" × 48"

spacers: 2 pieces of ¼" plywood, ¾" × 48"

paint: 1 spray can of light brown flat enamel

overhang gauge: 1 piece of ¾" plywood, 1" × 26"

mirror tiles: 4 packaged, precut mirror tiles 12" × 12"

I. Preparing the Base

Lay the plywood base on a flat surface with the short sides (26") to the right and left.

• Draw and label the following parallel lines across the plywood:

    A — 3" down from the top
    B — 6" down from the top
    C — 7" down from the top
    D — 19" down from the top
    E — 20" down from the top
    F — 23" down from the top

• Mark and label the following points, measuring from the left:

    4 — 12" in on the top edge
    5 — 24" in on the top edge
    6 — 36" in on the top edge
    2 — 3" in on line **A**
    3 — 15" in on line **A**
    7 — 33" in on line **A**
    8 — 45" in on line **A**
    1 — 6" in on line **B**
    9 — 42" in on line **B**
    10 — 6" in on line **E**
    18 — 42" in on lne **E**
    11 — 3" in on line **F**
    12 — 15" in on line **F**
    16 — 33" in on line **F**
    17 — 45" in on line **F**
    13 — 12" in on the bottom edge
    14 — 24" in on the bottom edge
    15 — 36" in on the bottom edge

Note on Materials

You can find packaged, precut mirror tiles at most hardware stores.

- Draw lines between the following pairs of points:

  4 and 3

  2 and 1

  13 and 12

  11 and 10

  6 and 7

  8 and 9

  15 and 16

  17 and 18

Center one ¾" × 48" spacer between lines **B** and **C** and the other between lines **D** and **E**. Using 1" paneling nails, nail the spacers in place every 4" at these locations.

Now, cut out the mirror frame with a saw. Paint the top and bottom (including the spacers) and the edges of the plywood brown.

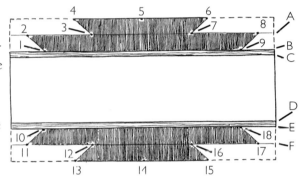

2. Installing the Center Trim

Draw a line through the center of the base from point **5** to point **14**. Starting at this center line, use a protractor to draw 45-degree lines, as illustrated on page 116, about every three inches. These reference lines will help you keep the trim at the right angle.

Center and then tack the overhang gauge across the top edge of the plywood base with 8d nails. Cut a 45-degree angle on one end of a 12" center trim piece. Place this center trim piece so that it slightly overhangs the left upper side edge of the base, with the 45-degree angle butted against the top spacer. Hold the piece in place and mark the other end at the outside edge of the overhang gauge. Remove the trim piece and cut this end square across on the mark. Put the trim piece back in place, making sure it parallels and slightly overhangs the edge of the plywood. Then drill three $\frac{1}{16}$" pilot holes, one near each end and one in the center, and nail this trim piece in place with 1" paneling nails.

Moving to the right, repeat this process until you reach the center line. Then move to the *right* side of the base and work in toward the center line in the same manner. Be sure the first piece on the right side also parallels and overhangs the edge.

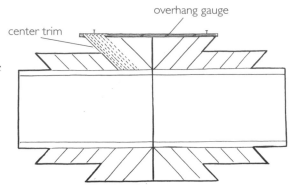

Note on Pilot Holes

Drill all pilot holes for this project with a $\frac{1}{16}$" bit unless otherwise specified. (The deck screws in step 5 require $\frac{1}{8}$" pilot holes.)

3. Installing the Herringbone Trim

You will create a herringbone pattern to complete the top of the frame, beginning at the base of the V formed by the inner center trim pieces. Start by alternating pieces on the left and the right, butting them against each other in the center. *Cut all pieces square on both ends.* Trim off the ends squarely at the outside edge of the overhang gauge. The center line should meet the inside corner of the herringbone when an equal number of pieces are placed on each side. If you need to adjust the alignment, try pieces having slightly larger or smaller diameters. When all the herringbone pieces fit properly, drill and nail as you did the center trim.

For the final trim piece, install a small triangle of willow to cover the edge of the plywood base. You may need to split a piece of trim in half to use here. Repeat steps 2 and 3 for the bottom of the base.

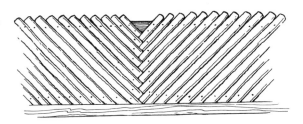

4. Installing the Edge Trim

Move the overhang gauge to the top edge of the plywood on the side where you plan to begin installing the edge trim. (You may cut the overhang gauge in half, to 13", to make it less awkward to work with.) Then tack it across the edge of the plywood with 8d nails.

Cut a 45-degree angle on one end of a 7" edge trim piece. Place the piece next to the center trim with the 45-degree angle butted against the spacer. Hold the piece in place and mark the other end at the outside edge of the overhang gauge. Remove the piece and cut this end square across on the mark. Put the trim piece back in place, drill two pilot holes, 1" from the ends, and nail it in place. Continue nailing trim on until you are about four pieces from the end.

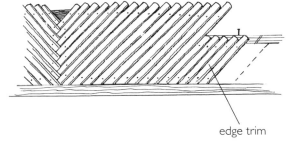

edge trim

Before you nail the last four pieces on, lay them in place and see if they will cover the plywood sufficiently. Also confirm that the final piece will overhang the edge but can still be nailed to the plywood. If not, choose different diameter pieces until you get the correct coverage. Then drill pilot holes and nail these pieces in place.

Repeat this process on the other side.

Now, repeat all of step 4 for the bottom of the base.

5. Assembling the Mirror Trim

For the two horizontal mirror trim pieces, select willow limbs that are as straight as possible. Lay each so that it covers as much of a spacer as possible, with the most attractive side up. Center the pieces, drill ⅛" pilot holes (one in the center and one on each end 2" in from the edge of the plywood), and screw them to the plywood base with 2" deck screws. You may need to flex the limb and use additional screws in some places to cover the spacers better.

Measuring from one side of the plywood base, lightly mark the top of both horizontal mirror trim pieces at 12", 24", and 36". Next, measure the distance between the horizontal mirror trim pieces at each location you marked and cut vertical mirror trim pieces to fit. A rounded T-joint works well here (see chapter 2, page 30, for how to make a rounded T-joint). Cut two additional pieces of vertical mirror trim to overlap the left and right edges of the plywood base.

Leaving enough clearance for the mirror tiles that you will install between the plywood base and the vertical trim, drill ⅛" pilot holes through the horizontal trim pieces into the ends of the vertical trim pieces. Fasten with 3" deck screws.

Now unscrew the mirror trim assembly from the plywood base so you can install the mirror tiles.

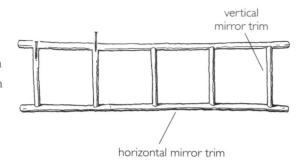

vertical mirror trim

horizontal mirror trim

6. Completing the Mirror

Attach the mirror tiles to the plywood base following the manufacturer's instructions. Place the first piece on the left flush with the edge of the plywood and the bottom edge of the top spacer. Butt the other three tiles next to each other, in line.

Set the mirror trim assembly back in place on top of the spacers. Position it carefully over the mirror tiles and screw it in place. *To avoid breaking the mirror tiles, do not overtighten the screws.*

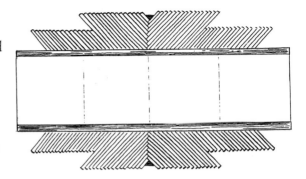

Log Cabin Planter Box

This is a popular, versatile, very sturdy willow design. Right side up, it makes a great planter box out on the porch; turned upside down, it's a perfect porch end table. We used threaded rod in our design to pin the logs, which adds strength and allows you to adjust the stack as the logs dry out.

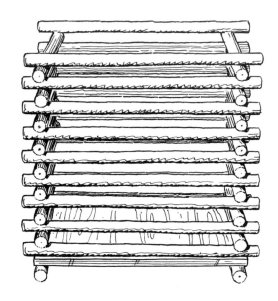

Materials				
Part	Quantity	Diameter	Length	Type of Wood
logs	30	1"	20"	seasoned
bottom cap logs	2	1"	20"	seasoned
top cap logs	2	1"	20"	seasoned
trim logs	2	1"	20"	seasoned

bottom: 1 piece of ¾" *exterior* plywood, 18" × 18"

paint: 1 spray can of dark brown flat enamel

rod: 4 pieces of ¼" threaded rod, 18" long

washers: 8 plain washers, ¼"

nuts: 4 plain nuts, ¼"; 4 cap nuts, ¼"

1. Preparing the Bottom

Draw a line ¾" in from the edge of the plywood bottom on all sides. At the corners, where the lines intersect, drill a ⁵⁄₁₆" hole. Then paint the plywood bottom dark brown.

Put one washer and then one plain nut on each threaded rod. Insert the other end of each rod up through one of the a holes in the plywood bottom. Set the bottom on a flat surface with the rods standing up.

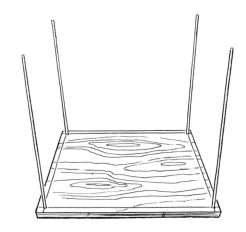

2. Stacking the Logs

Sort the logs for the sides by diameters. As you build the box, use larger or smaller diameter pieces and mix thick and thin ends to keep the height of the parallel sides as uniform as you can. Lay the pieces on a flat surface and roll them around to find the flattest side. With this side down, measure 1¾" in from each end of the thirty log pieces and mark the center. Make sure the paired marks are in line.

Place each log on scrap wood and drill a ⁵⁄₁₆" hole through on each mark. Then round the edges with a file or Surform plane.

Place the first two logs on the threaded rods on parallel sides, and then seat two more on the other two sides. Continue placing the rest of the logs on the rods in log-cabin style.

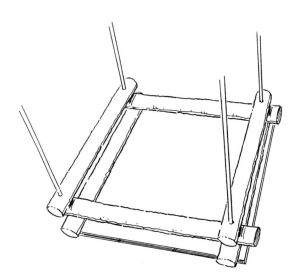

3. Capping the Top

As you did for the side logs, measure 1¾" in from each end of the top cap log pieces and mark the center. Make sure the marks are in line. Drill a ⁵⁄₁₆" hole through on each mark. Round the edges with a file or Surform plane.

Lay a washer over each one of the holes you drilled and mark its outline on the log. Remove the washer and chisel or whittle the space around the drilled holes to the depth of the washers. Remove enough wood so the washers will lay flat with the surface of the log.

Place the top cap logs on the threaded rod with the chiseled side out. Put a washer and a cap nut on each rod. Tighten the four cap nuts while holding the rod with a pair of pliers. Hammer the threaded rod back through the logs until the washers are fully seated in the chiseled holes and the cap nuts are tight against them. An inch or so of rod should now protrude at the bottom of the box. Lay the planter box on its side and hand-tighten the four plain nuts. Square up the box, then hold the cap nut and tighten the plain nuts with a wrench or pliers. Tighten each nut a little at a time, working your way around the box to avoid distorting the square shape. Before you finish tightening all of the nuts, check the box again to make sure it is square and straight.

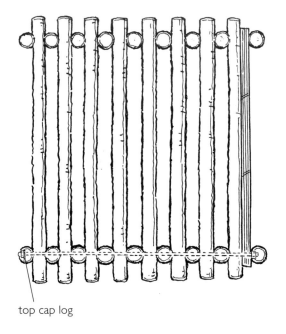

top cap log

4. Capping the Bottom

Set the planter box on a flat surface with the plywood bottom up. Using a hacksaw, trim off the excess threaded rod even with the plain nuts.

Measure in 1¼" and 2¼" from each end of the bottom cap log pieces. Mark these locations and draw inch-long connecting lines between the pairs of marks. Chisel or whittle the wood along this line, making a cavity in the cap log deep enough to cover the washer and nut at the plywood bottom. Remove enough material so the bottom cap logs will lay flat against the bottom. Round the edges of each cap log with a file or Surform plane.

Position the bottom cap logs to continue the log cabin design. Drill ³⁄₃₂" pilot holes and nail the bottom cap logs to the plywood bottom with 8d nails.

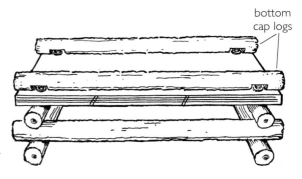

bottom cap logs

5. Installing the Trim Logs

Round the edges of the two trim pieces with a file or Surform plane. Set the planter box upright on a flat surface. Measure in 1¾" from each end of the trim log pieces and mark the center.

Choose a ½" spade or paddle bit. Wrap a piece of electrician's or other tape around the bit, ½" up from the tip. Drill a hole at each mark on the trim logs, *stopping when the tape touches the wood.*

Place the trim logs across the planter box, continuing the log cabin design. The countersunk holes should completely cover the cap nut. At each end of the trim logs drill a ³⁄₃₂" pilot hole at an angle that misses the cap nuts. Nail the trim logs to the top cap log with 8d nails.

trim logs

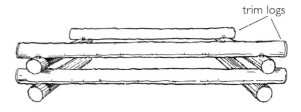

Tightening the Box

After the willow fully dries, you may need to tighten the box. If so, remove the bottom cap logs, adjust the four plain nuts, trim off the excess rod with a hacksaw, and then replace the cap logs.

# Decorative
Wheelbarrow Plant Stand

This wheelbarrow plant stand can be used indoors or outdoors on the patio or in the yard to display your favorite plants. With flowering pots arranged on the bed, it looks great on our lawn in the summer. In the winter, we move it near the entry door to hold wet boots.

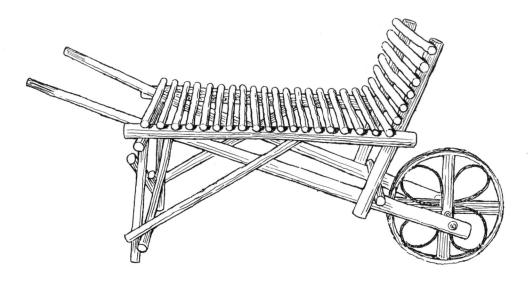

Materials				
Part	Quantity	Diameter	Length	Type of Wood
rim benders	4	½"	58	flexible
spokes	2	1½"	cut to fit	seasoned
trim	4	⅜"	approx. 28"	flexible
legs	2	1½"	17½"	seasoned
top support	1	1½"	24"	seasoned
cross braces	2	1½"	24"	seasoned
filler	1	1½"	6"	seasoned
handles	2	2"	60"	seasoned
front support	1	1½"	18"	seasoned
rail supports	2	2"	24"	seasoned
rails	2	2"	36"	seasoned
temporary brace	1	1"	19"	seasoned
slats	25	1"	24"	seasoned
bottom braces	2	1½"	approx. 27"	seasoned

template: 2 pieces of ¾" plywood, 18" × 18"

pipe: 1 piece of ¼" galvanized pipe, 3" long

rod: 1 piece of 5⁄16" threaded steel rod, 12" long

washers: 6 fender (large area) washers, 5⁄16"

nuts: 6 plain nuts, 5⁄16"; 2 lock nuts, 5⁄16"

I. Beginning the Wheel

Draw lines diagonally from corner to corner to find the center of a plywood template. Take a piece of scrap wood 10" to 12" long, and drive a nail through 8" from one end. Place the protruding nail point on the center of a template and drive it in just enough to allow the scrap piece to pivot.

Hold a pencil against the 8" end of the scrap and draw a circle on the template. Discard the scrap piece. Then choose one of the diagonal lines and mark it. On the circumference of the circle, at points 2" to each side of this diagonal line, drive in a 6d nail, for a total of four nails. Drive additional 6d nails into the plywood every 3" to 4" along the circumference. These nails will hold the rim benders as they dry in the template.

Place the thick end of one of the rim benders between the nails that flank the diagonal line you marked, with 3" of the bender extending outside the circle. Wrap the rim bender inside the circle of nails. When you return to your starting point, lay the bender across the thick end and let it extend outside the circle. You may need to place additional nails on the inside of the bender to maintain a round shape.

Create a second template and repeat this process for another rim bender.

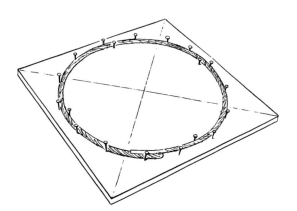

Limbering Benders

Remember, it's easier to work with flexible benders if you limber them up before you attach them. Stretching the wood fibers makes the benders more pliable and much easier to bend. For how to limber willow, see chapter 1.

2. Making the Spokes

Measure the length of the marked diagonal line inside the rim bender. Cut a spoke to this length and center the ends on the diagonal line. Holding the bender and spoke against the plywood, drill $\frac{1}{16}$" pilot holes and carefully nail the thick end of the rim bender to the spoke with two $1\frac{5}{8}$" paneling nails. Remember to stagger the nails so you don't split the end. Now trim off the thick end of the rim bender $\frac{1}{2}$" beyond the spoke.

Make sure the spoke is centered on the diagonal line. Then drill two ¹⁄₁₆" pilot holes and nail the other end of the rim bender to the spoke. Trim it off ½" beyond the spoke. Drill two ¹⁄₁₆" holes through the rim bender into the other end of the spoke and nail them together.

Repeat this step for the second spoke, using the second template.

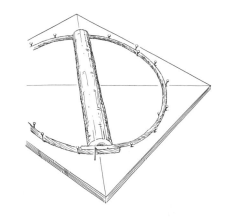

3. Completing the Wheel Halves

Lay another rim bender on top of the first rim bender in one of the templates. Begin this bender at the opposite end of the marked diagonal line. Again, place the thick end between the nails that flank the diagonal, with 3" of the bender extending outside the circle. Wrap the rim bender inside the circle of nails, drill pilot holes, fasten it to the spoke, and trim as you did the first rim bender. At 4" intervals round the circle, drill ¹⁄₁₆" pilot holes and nail the benders together with 1" paneling nails. Leave the assembled wheel half in the template for three days, and then remove it.

Repeat this step using the fourth rim bender, in the second template.

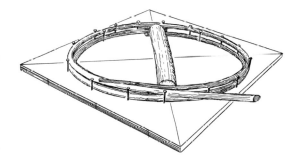

4. Finishing the Wheel

Place the flatter sides of the wheel halves together on a flat surface, with the spokes perpendicular.

Moving clockwise, drill 1/16" pilot holes in the rim benders 2½" past each spoke, and nail with 1⅝" paneling nails as you go. Flip the wheel assembly over and repeat this process on the other side.

Now, drill a ½" hole all the way through the center of the spokes where they cross. Insert the 3" piece of galvanized pipe in this hole and drive it in flush with the spoke.

Drill a 1/16" pilot hole and, using 1" paneling nails, and nail the center of a trim piece to the inside of the rim in the middle of one of the four wheel quadrants, halfway between the spokes. Bend the trim piece to the center of the wheel; drill 1/16" pilot holes in the trim and spokes, 1" from the ends, near where the spokes meet; and nail the trim to the spokes with 1" paneling nails. Trim off the excess length.

Repeat this process to trim all four wheel quadrants.

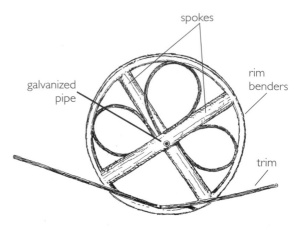

spokes

rim benders

galvanized pipe

trim

5. Beginning the Leg and Brace Assembly

Measure in 3½" from each end of the top support piece and drill ⅛" in-line pilot holes all the way through. Drill another pilot hole in the center of one end of both legs. Nail the top support piece to the legs with 16d nails.

Lay the top support and leg assembly on a flat surface with the open (bottom) end toward you, and adjust the legs until they are square with the top support. Measure up from the bottom of the legs 6" and 15", marking the outside edge of the legs at both locations.

Mark both cross braces 1½" from their top ends. Lay the first brace diagonally across the legs, lining up the mark on the brace with the top mark you made on the right leg. Also, line up the brace with the lower mark on the left leg, as illustrated.

Center a ⅛" pilot hole where the cross brace and the right leg intersect. Nail the two together with a 16d nail. Square the assembly, and then, as before, drill and nail the cross brace and the left leg.

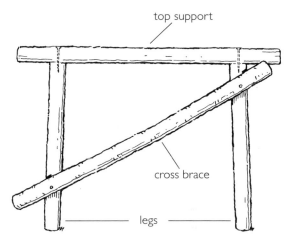

6. Finishing the Leg and Brace Assembly

Flip this assembly over, keeping the open end of the legs toward you. Mark the center of the cross brace you just installed.

Measure in 1½" from each end of the filler piece and drill ⅛" in-line pilot holes. Align the center of the filler piece with the center mark you just made on the cross brace. Holding the filler and brace firmly, drill back through the filler holes and slightly into the cross brace. Remove the filler piece and deepen the pilot holes in the cross brace. Now, nail the filler to the brace with 16d nails.

Lay the second cross brace diagonally across the legs and filler piece, again lining up the mark on the cross brace with the top mark on what is now the right leg. Also, line up the brace with the lower mark on the left leg, as illustrated. Drill a ⅛" pilot hole where the cross brace and the right leg intersect, and nail these pieces together with a 16d nail. Square the assembly, and then, as before, drill and nail the cross brace and the left leg.

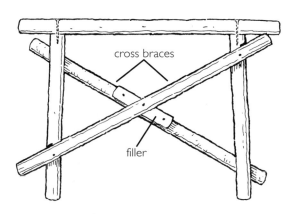

Finally, drill a ⅛" pilot hole through the center of the cross brace and the center of the filler piece, and nail them together with a 16d nail.

7. Making the Handles

Drill a ⅛" pilot hole 13" from the *thicker* end of each handle piece. Drill a second ⅛" in-line pilot hole 16" from the other end of each handle. Also drill ⅛" in-line pilot holes 4" from each end of the front support piece. Now, using 16d nails, nail the front support to the handles through the first set of pilot holes you drilled (the ones 13" from the ends).

To attach the handles to the leg and brace assembly, begin by measuring in 3¼" from each end of the top support piece and drilling a ⅛" pilot hole through the top. Lay the handles across the top support, *making sure the front support piece on the handles is up.* Line up the handles' second set of pilot holes (the ones 16" from the ends) with the holes you just drilled in the top support. Nail the handle to the top support with 16d nails.

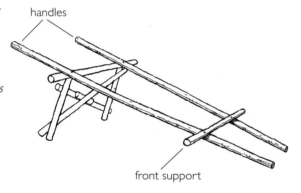

handles

front support

8. Attaching the Rail Supports to the Handles

Drill a ⅛" pilot hole 13" from the top end of a rail support. Drill another ⅛" in-line pilot hole 1½" from the bottom end.

Now, slide the bottom end of the rail support down the outside of either handle, until it rests flush against the front support piece and perpendicular to the handle. Centering the hole in the rail support against the handle, drill back through the hole and slightly into the handle. Remove the rail support and deepen the hole. Then reposition the rail support and nail it to the handle with a 16d nail.

Repeat this process with the other rail support, nailing it to the other handle.

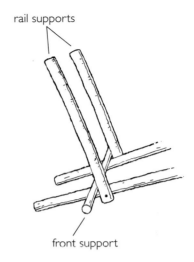

rail supports

front support

9. Completing the Bed

Drill ⅛" in-line pilot holes 2½" in from each end of a rail. Align one of the holes with the upper hole you previously drilled in either rail support. Nail the rail to the outside of the rail support with a 16d nail.

Center the hole in the other end of the rail above the top support, then drill back through the hole and slightly into the handle. Lift the rail out of the way and deepen the pilot hole. Nail the rail to the handle with a 16d nail.

Repeat this process for the other rail, nailing it to the other handle.

Standing at the front of the wheelbarrow, adjust the rail supports until they are straight vertically. Then drill a ⅛" pilot hole through the front support into each rail support, and nail with 16d nails.

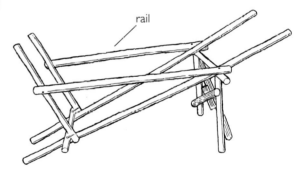

rail

10. Installing the First Flats

Using 8d nails, tack the temporary brace piece diagonally to one leg and handle to keep the leg assembly from moving around when you nail the slats on.

Center the first slat across the rails, tight against the rail supports. Drill ⅛" pilot holes through the slat into the rails and nail it to the rails with 6d nails. Position the next slat where the handle meets the rails; drill and nail as you did for the first slat.

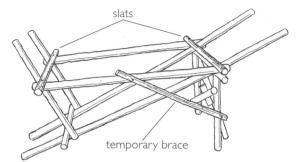

slats

temporary brace

I I. Completing the Slats

Using 6d nails, tack a straight piece of scrap wood to one side of the wheelbarrow, on the outside ends of the first two slats. This piece is a temporary guide to help you keep the slat ends in line.

Use two scrap pieces of plywood or other material about ¾" thick to space the slats evenly. Drill pilot holes and nail slats across the bed, beginning next to the first slat and butting them to the guide, until you are about four pieces away from the second slat you installed. As you proceed, check a few times to be sure the slats are parallel across the bed. Make adjustments by using slats with larger or smaller diameters. Before you nail the last four pieces, lay them in place and see if they will cover the space sufficiently. If not, choose slats with different diameters until you get the correct coverage, and then nail these in place.

Repeat this process up the front of the wheelbarrow, again using a straight piece of scrap wood as a guide and nailing the slats to the rail supports. Remove the guide when you finish.

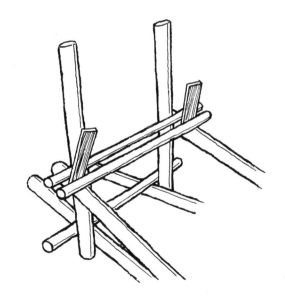

I2. Mounting the Wheel

Turn the wheelbarrow upside down on a flat surface. Measure in 2" from the front end of the handles and mark the outside of each so that a line drawn between the two marks would run parallel to the front support. Drill a ⅜" hole through each handle on the mark, *making sure that the holes are in line with each other.*

Insert one end of the threaded steel rod through one handle, and then place a washer and three plain nuts on the rod on the inside of the handle. Thread the nuts onto the rod about 2", and then add another washer.

Position the wheel between the handles and insert the rod through the wheel until about 2" sticks out the other side. Now put a washer on the rod, and then the other three plain nuts and another washer.

Feeding the rod through the handle on this side, place another washer and a lock nut on the outside of the handle.

I3. Securing the Wheel

A. To hold the rod while tightening the first lock nut, begin by tightening against each other the two plain nuts nearest the wheel on the same side as the lock nut. Then hold the nut nearest the wheel with a wrench and tighten the lock nut until the end of the rod is flush with the outside of the nut.

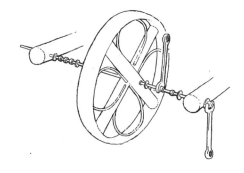

B. Loosen the two plain nuts you tightened against each other and secure that side's third plain nut against the handle. *Do not overtighten.*

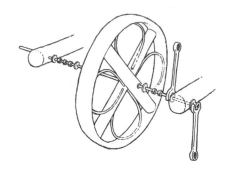

C. Now put the final washer and the second lock nut on the other end of the rod. Repeat steps A and B to secure the other handle. However, stop tightening the lock nut when the washer contacts the handle. This will leave some of the threaded rod sticking out past the lock nut.

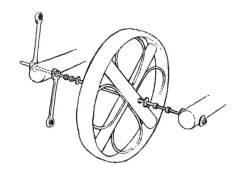

D. Once the handles are secured, further loosen the plain nuts that were tightened against each other (if necessary) and center the wheel between the handles. Finger-tighten the plain nuts nearest the wheel on each side. Hold one of these plain nuts with a wrench and tighten the adjacent nut against it. Now loosen the nut on the other side of the wheel ½ turn. Holding this nut secure with a wrench, spin the wheel to be sure it turns freely. Tighten or loosen this nut as needed to allow the wheel to spin without binding, and then tighten the adjacent nut to lock the wheel in place. Finally, cut the excess rod off with a hacksaw.

14. Installing the Bottom Braces

Turn the wheelbarrow upright on a flat surface. Remove the temporary brace you installed at the beginning of step 10. Step back and look at the legs. They should be straight. Adjust them now if you need to (firm, quick pushes from side to side will allow you to straighten the legs).

Mark the side of the handles 30" up from the front. Lay one of the bottom braces on the mark, outside the leg and with the bottom edge resting on top of the cross brace. Butt the top end of the brace against the rail and mark the angle of the rail on the brace. Cut the brace to fit snugly against the rail.

Put the bottom brace back in place and drill a ⅛" pilot hole through the brace into the handle. Nail with a 16d nail. Make sure the legs remain straight. Now, drill a ⅛" pilot hole through the bottom brace into the leg, and nail with a 16d nail. Drill a ³⁄₃₂" pilot hole through the bottom brace into the rail and nail with a 6d nail.

Repeat this process to install the second bottom brace on the other side.

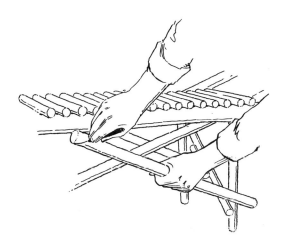

Finishing Touch

To give the wheelbarrow handles a hewn and worn look, shape the last 8" or so with a Surform plane, spoke shave, or draw knife to fit your hands.

 # Finish and Care

Let willow furniture season for 3 to 6 weeks out of direct sunlight. Natural, unfinished wood furniture used indoors requires only an occasional dusting and light oiling with any fine furniture oil. Or you can tint your furniture to match the predominant wood in your decor and finish it to be used indoors or out.

Aging the Wood

You can age new wood to look like old barn wood with a solution of vinegar and steel wool. Shred a pad or a golf-ball-sized piece of very fine steel wool and drop it into a quart of white vinegar. Drill some holes in the cap of the vinegar bottle. Then set the bottle in direct sunlight for about three days. The vinegar will dissolve the steel wool.

Test the concentration of the solution by dipping in a wood toothpick or other small piece of wood. When the wood turns the color you want, strain the solution through two coffee filters and pour it into a spray bottle. Spray the solution onto the wood and wipe off the excess with an old, clean cloth to prevent streaking.

Allow the wood to dry and then apply additional coats if you want a darker color. Be careful when handling or spraying this solution. It will stain whatever it touches, including your hands!

Dyeing

Willow can be dyed to create interesting variations in your designs. Stripped of the bark, willow is a light blonde color that dyes very well (see chapter 2, page 20, for how to strip the bark). You can also experiment with sponge dyeing pieces that have the bark left on. The bark of most willow species dries like a tight skin around the wood. Dye a branch of your wood to test the effect before you dye the entire piece. You can dye small pieces in a plastic bucket or a bathtub, but you will have to sponge dye larger pieces.

Using a Dye Bath

You can use RIT dye (available in most supermarkets) or basketry dyes found in most craft supply stores. To prepare RIT dye for small pieces that will be immersed in a plastic bucket or bathtub, plan on two packages of dye for every 1 gallon of water. Begin by completely dissolving one package in 1 pint of hot water. Mix your dye solution in a quart jar, and then thin the solution by adding it to more hot water. Otherwise, you may end up with splotches of darker color from pieces of undissolved powder. Never pour the dye directly on the piece — it can cause uneven, blotchy coloring.

When your dye bath is ready, immerse the willow pieces and move them constantly back and forth to avoid streaking. Continue this process for 15 to 20 minutes or until you get the desired shade. If you want a darker shade, add more dye solution and continue the process.

Take the pieces out of the dye bath and let them set for 10 minutes. Then rinse them thoroughly in *cold* water. This is an important step: It helps set the dye and also washes off the excess, so it won't rub off on your clothes later.

Sponge Dyeing

To sponge dye larger pieces, set them in the middle of a large plastic drop cloth spread on the floor. Mix your dye solution in a quart jar and then pour it into a plastic bucket. (For RIT, use one package of dye to 1 pint of *hot* water.). You can add more dye if you want a more intense shade.

Using a large sponge, wipe the dye onto the piece. Smooth and blend the color until you get the even shade you want. Let the dye set for 10 minutes, then rinse the piece thoroughly with *cold* water. In addition to removing excess dye, a good rinsing also helps work the dye into crevices. Let the piece dry completely, and then apply finish coats of polyurethane or varnish.

Matching Golden Oak

If the predominant wood in your decor is golden oak, give your willow pieces a matching glow and seal them for outdoor use by tinting with a mixture of 50 percent Golden Oak Watco Danish Oil Finish and 50 percent tung oil. Either spray or brush this mixture on in a well-ventilated area. Turn the piece upside down and coat underneath also. Apply generous amounts to all cut ends, frame, and benders. Let the furniture dry for about 3 days in a dust-free area out of direct sunlight. Apply a coat of 100 percent tung oil each spring before you put your furniture back outside, and it will last for many years.

Painting

Willow furniture can be painted to match any decor. Set the piece in the middle of a large drop cloth in an open area and gather your paint supplies. You'll need:

- 2 or 3 paint brushes of different sizes
- sandpaper, fine and very fine grades
- old cotton rags
- small plastic containers for the paint
- acrylic primer or acrylic gesso
- artist's acrylic paint, the colors of your choice

Wipe the furniture down with hot soapy water to remove any dirt or dust, and let it dry completely. Then vacuum the piece with an upholstery attachment or wipe it down with a soft brush to remove any tiny particles.

Next, apply a base coat of acrylic gesso or acrylic primer. Brush on two light coats or one heavy coat, and let it dry. Lightly sand the piece with a fine grade of sandpaper, and wipe it down with a clean dry cloth to remove any sanding dust. This base coat provides a good foundation for the paint and makes the colors more vivid.

Apply the first coat of acrylic paint and let the piece dry completely. Add on a second coat if any of the primer shows through.

Instead of painting your piece with one solid color, you might want to try one of the following variations.

Applying Finishes

After painting, finish coat your piece with acrylic matte varnish for a more natural look, or a semigloss varnish for a more modern, glossy look. For outdoor furniture, it's a good idea to apply a new coat of varnish each spring, before you put it back outside.

Dry Brushing

You can create a highlighted look by dry brushing a contrasting color on top of the first coat of paint. Use a medium-size, dry paint brush. Dip the brush in the contrasting color and paint a piece of newspaper until only a small amount of paint remains in the brush. Apply the paint to the furniture with fast, light strokes. Dry brushing highlights the outer ridges of the wood, adding depth and dimension to your piece.

As a variation, you can highlight the arms and rounded back of a chair or loveseat using this dry-brush technique. Then paint the seat and back slats in solid colors, alternating the contrasting colors.

Antiquing

If you like the antique look, apply one coat of color onto the piece. Let it dry for a day or two, and then sand the piece with very fine sandpaper until some of the wood shows through.

Spatter Painting

If you make a piece for a child's room, you might want to try spatter painting. Apply two coats of paint to the furniture and let them dry completely. Then choose two contrasting colors and spatter them onto the piece. Use a dry brush with small amounts of paint.

Spatter painting can be quite messy but a lot of fun. Be sure you spatter paint on a large drop cloth in an open area away from other furniture.

# Other Storey Titles You Will Enjoy

Deckscaping, by Barbara W. Ellis. Use your deck in more in any season. Barbara Ellis sets out to improve the appearance and comfort of any needy deck. She suggests surfaces, lighting, plantings, and furniture — from simple to elaborate — and gives tips on maintenance. 176 pages. Paperback. ISBN 1-58017-408-6.

Garden Stone, by Barbara Pleasant. Practical information and more than 250 inspiring photographs explain how to use stone and plants together to create contrasting textures and colors in the garden. Stone projects are clearly described and gardeners will appreciate helpful tips on growing plants in paths and stone walls. 240 pages. Hardcover. ISBN 1-58017-406-X.

Making Bentwood Trellises, Arbors, Gates, and Fences, by Jim Long. A companion volume in The Rustic Home Series. Learn how to make your garden or landscape more romantic and inviting with the addition of a trellis, arbor, or natural fence. Includes step-by-step instructions on how to collect limbs from a wide variety of native trees and then craft and install dozens of trellis, gate, arbor, and fence designs. 144 pages. Features 16 pages of full-color photography. Paperback. ISBN 1-58017-051-X.

Poolscaping, by Catriona Tudor Erler. Transform your pool and the surrounding area into the welcoming and appealing focal point of your home's outdoor living space. Gardener and landscape designer Catriona Tudor Erler takes readers step-by-step through the poolscaping process — siting the pool; designing the surrounding edging; choosing lighting and fencing; and finally picking the best poolside plants, with a focus on varieties that are low maintenance , look attractive throughout the season, and won't drop leaves into the water. Includes ideas for planters and containers to bring greenery and color right up to the water's edge. 208 pages. Hardcover ISBN 1-58017-386-1. Paperback. ISBN 1-58017-385-3.

Stonework: Techniques and Projects, by Charles McRaven. This complete guide includes fully illustrated, step-by-step instructions for 22 attractive projects, including walls, porches, pools, seats, waterfalls, and even a bridge. Advice on gathering and handling stone and hiring stonemasons is also included. 192 pages. Paperback. ISBN 0-88266-976-1.

These and other Storey books are available wherever books are sold and directly from
Storey Publishing, 210 MASS MoCA Way, North Adams, MA 01247, or by calling 1-800-441-5700.
Visit our website at www.storey.com.